GAME FISHING

By the same author

Begin Fishing with Uncle Bill
Freshwater Fishing
Sea Fishing
The Fish We Catch
Places to Fish
Fly Dressing and Some Tackle Making

Also available as Paperfronts

GAME FISHING

TROUT–SALMON–SEA TROUT

Written and illustrated by

W. E. (BILL) DAVIES

PAPERFRONTS

ELLIOT RIGHT WAY BOOKS
KINGSWOOD, SURREY UK

Made and printed in Great Britain by C. Nicholls & Company Ltd, The Philips Park Press ,Manchester.

To
Hilda, My Wife

CONTENTS

Chapter		Page
1	Introduction	11
2	Natural History of Brown Trout	15
3	Habits of Brown Trout	20
4	Trout and the Weather	26
5	Nature's Signposts	28
6	Which Fly?	32
7	Using the Sunken Fly	39
8	Loch and Lake Fishing	46
9	Nymph Fishing	50
10	Dry-Fly Fishing	55
11	Up-stream Worming	61
12	Creeper Fishing	67
13	Using Live Insects	71
14	Spinning Technique	76
15	Which Fly? Which District?	82
16	Re-stocking Trout Streams	85
17	Care of Tackle	91
18	The Rainbow Trout	95
19	The Salmon	102
20	Natural History of Salmon and a Few Perils	105
21	Identifying the Catch	113
22	Is it a Kelt?	116
23	Locating the Best Lies	119
24	Tackle Problems	124
25	Fly Fishing	127
26	Using the Floating Line	135
27	Bait Fishing	139
28	Using Artificial Baits	144
29	Foiling the Poacher	150
30	Cooking the Catch	154

Chapter		Page
31	Natural History of Sea Trout	157
32	Fly Fishing for Sea Trout	163
33	The Fly at Night	167
34	Estuary Fishing	171
35	Worm Fishing	175
36	The Mysterious Bull Trout	178
37	Inexpensive Fishing for Your Holiday	182
38	Odds and Ends	184
	Ten Commandments	186
	Index	187

LIST OF ILLUSTRATIONS

		Page
Fig. 1	Birth of a Trout	15
Fig. 2	Enemies of Young Trout	17
Fig. 3	Brown Trout	21
Fig. 4	Some Insects Trout Love	22
Fig. 5	Haunts of Big Trout	24
Fig. 6	Swallow – One of Nature's Signposts	30
Fig. 7	Mayflies and Dry-Flies	34
Fig. 8	Six Good Wet-Flies	35
Fig. 9	Six Spider Flies	36
Fig. 10	How to Dress a Fly Correctly	37
Fig. 11	Amadou Fungus	44
Fig. 12	Scottish Loch Trout	46
Fig. 13	Nymphs and Other Artificials	51
Fig. 14	Example of Trout Feeding Area	56
Fig. 15	A Comfortable Grip on the Rod	57
Fig. 16	Knots and Worms	62
Fig. 17	Ideal Up-stream Worming Water	65
Fig. 18	An Ideal Spot for Creeper Fishing	68
Fig. 19	Overhung Pools are Ideal for Caterpillars	74
Fig. 20	Spinning Baits	78
Fig. 21	Underwater Animal Life	87
Fig. 22	Good Weeds	88
Fig. 23	Winter Chores	94
Fig. 24	Rainbow Trout	96
Fig. 25	Black Streamer Fly	98
Fig. 26	Hatching Olive Nymph	99
Fig. 27	Black and Peacock Beetle	100
Fig. 28	Dambuster	101
Fig. 29	Salmon Leaping a Waterfall	106
Fig. 30	A Salmon	107

Fig. 31 How to Distinguish between Salmon Parr and Young Trout 110
Fig. 32 A Natural Fish Ladder 111
Fig. 33 What a Tail can Tell 114
Fig. 34 Gill-Cover Identification 115
Fig. 35 Identifying a Kelt 117
Fig. 36 Where Salmon Lie in Rivers 120
Fig. 37 Salmon Lies in a Loch 122
Fig. 38 Some Famous Salmon Flies 128
Fig. 39 A Safe Knot for Nylon Leaders and Traces 130
Fig. 40 Occasional Flies 131
Fig. 41 Shrimps and Grubs 133
Fig. 42 Low-Water and Dry-Flies 137
Fig. 43 Natural Baits for Spinning 140
Fig. 44 Hooks for Worming 142
Fig. 45 Spoons for Salmon 145
Fig. 46 Devons 147
Fig. 47 Feathers, Hair and Plastic Baits for Spinning Rods 148
Fig. 48 A "Forbes Strachan" Netting Spoiler 152
Fig. 49 Sea Trout 158
Fig. 50 River Lies of Sea Trout 159
Fig. 51 Loch Lomond 161
Fig. 52 Sea Trout Flies and Spiders 164
Fig. 53 Sea Trout Demons and Terrors 168
Fig. 54 Cast-Holder for Night Fishing 169
Fig. 55 The Author's Black Fly 172
Fig. 56 The Right Way with Worm 176
Fig. 57 Pauperhaugh Bridge Pool 178

1

INTRODUCTION

In the journey from boyhood well towards old age it is natural that a game-fish angling pilgrim should pick up, here and there, a little knowledge about the sport and the creatures he seeks to outwit. Even so, Nature, in her wisdom, still jealously guards many of the secrets of her children, and while science has lifted the veil on some, others have defied all attempts at solving.

That fact alone places angling well ahead of other sports. You may have the finest set of rods and reels, together with boxes of flies and lures, and still fail to catch fish. Why? The answer is simple.

To man, the highest product of animal evolution, the strange behaviour of the more primitive creatures such as fish has always been a subject of fascinating conjecture – most of it unfortunately false. For man, despite his intellect (or perhaps because of it), cannot fully conceive the world of fish, a world differently perceived through radically different senses. With natural, if unscientific, self-esteem, he often fails to appreciate the fine adjustment of lower creatures to the simple circumstances in which they live.

Some of the greatest anglers I have met have been shepherds and farmers, men who live their days close to Nature, and have studied the habits of her finny folk. To them tackle is of secondary importance.

Let me amplify this point. A few years ago, with the flush of success still on my brow in having won a keenly contested trout fishing competition, I took a holiday in the Highlands of Scotland. On the River Garry I came across an aged shepherd fishing. His creel was heavy with good trout, yet I had fished hard and only had one fish to show for it. I was using flies dressed on 14 and 16 hooks, the shepherd on No. 10s. The "flees ye are using are te sma", he said in answer to my query as to his success. I changed over to large No. 10 spider flies and started to catch good trout.

Apparently at that time of the year, September, there is a particularly heavy hatch of a large brown heather fly on which the trout feed almost exclusively.

In the main, anglers are a gregarious body, who are never more happy than when discussing the merits of a particular fly or bait, or the vagaries of the weather and its effects on their sport.

Some get into the habit, I am sorry to say, of blaming all manner of things for their failures. Of course, in minds powerfully predisposed for the conversion of ordinary into extraordinary occurrences, it may be readily conceived that the same spirit influences them in the many phases of angling. It is from such persons, when discussing the sport, that you often hear such expressions: "I have had a run of bad luck lately; "So and so always has good luck, but I was born to be unfortunate"; "This is not one of my good days", and so on. Others take the easy road out by blaming their tools, which is simply a case of a poor workman blaming the first thing that comes to mind, forgetting that it is he who operates the tools.

Now, however deluded such people may be by their own strong prepossessions, and however sincere in believing themselves, it occurs to me that in nineteen out of twenty cases, what is called good or bad luck is but the natural result of industry and judgement in one case, and carelessness and imprudence in the other, and that brings me to the subject of this book: Trout, salmon and sea trout fishing.

Throughout, I have tried to avoid scientific matters, believing that the ordinary angler has little time for them. It does not matter to him that the palatal and maxillary bones of the trout are stouter in comparison to those of a grayling. What he is concerned with is rising and eventually catching fish.

I have tried to describe the various ways of luring game fish. It may well be that some of my readers will not agree with certain of my theories. In passing judgement one must bear in mind that the last word on this sport of ours will never be written. Each year as my "education" advances I am forced to change my mind regarding some things. The angling cycle is like that. What is today is not tomorrow.

Scientists declare that the brain of a fish is very small. Be that as it may, we all know that it takes much brain-work on our part to outwit even a small trout. That is as it should be, for if we caught a bag of fish on every outing there would be no sport in it, and the thrill of expectancy when making the first cast of a season would vanish.

Impatience and muscle aren't what fill your bag. Use brains and take your time. After all, in addition to the purpose of catching fish, there are the very worthy inducements of environment, or fresh air, and the joy of careful observance of Nature in general. Too many of us forget that we are supposedly fishing for fun. Why make such a task of it? Why wear ourselves out physically until we are nothing but a bundle of raw nerves and aching muscles? Get the full measure of a day on the stream or lake by taking your time.

Today, as I look back over the years, I give thanks for the many friends I have made and for the patience they have exhibited towards me – an angling pilgrim.

My reason for placing trout first is simple, and when I say trout it includes brown as well as rainbow. Today there are more trout anglers than ever before. All over the country new reservoirs and lakes have been constructed. Owners of such waters, known by anglers as still waters, have a twin aim in so doing: attracting anglers and making money. It is big business.

Such man-made waters come in all sizes and shapes. Worked-out gravel pits are often converted into fishing centres. However, each particular water differs from the other in terrain, weather and water conditions. Some have one predominant fish, while others have several species, brown and rainbow trout mingling with freshwater fish (I hate the word coarse), such as tench, carp, rudd and roach.

Some man-made waters are quite shallow while others are deep or spread over many acres. However, fish with their innate instincts for survival do not differ in the north, south, east or west. Their behaviour does not vary in reservoirs from that in lakes, natural or man-made. Regardless of species, trout are trout no matter what their geographical location.

Years ago waters were usually stocked with brown trout. Today that species takes second place to the rainbow, which is an import from America. This brilliant-coloured trout has two important characteristics in its favour. First, it is not so prone to disease as the brown, and secondly, it grows much faster. As to its ability to extend the angler when hooked, I believe it to be more of a problem than the brown.

The popularity of the rainbow has been marked by the invention of many new flies, nymphs and lures. I have tested quite a few of them, and instructions on how to dress them are given in the chapter devoted to the rainbow.

However, while there are several chapters devoted to the brown trout, they could, generally speaking, relate to the rainbow as well. For instance, rods, reels, lines and leaders are the same under similar conditions and many flies that take brown trout also lure rainbows.

To prevent confusion in the mind of the reader, the early part of the book deals with trout and the later part, chapter 19 onwards, with salmon and sea trout.

What I have written will not guarantee a full bag at every outing, but I believe that if the hints given are used intelligently the words "luck" and "unlucky" will be heard less frequently.

2

NATURAL HISTORY OF BROWN TROUT

Trout usually spawn in October or November, the eggs being deposited on a bed of gravel. After about thirty days the eggs show signs of life, two brownish-black specks having appeared. At this stage they are termed eyed ova; forty to forty-five days later they hatch and a queer looking-little creature emerges called an alevin. It is absolutely helpless and

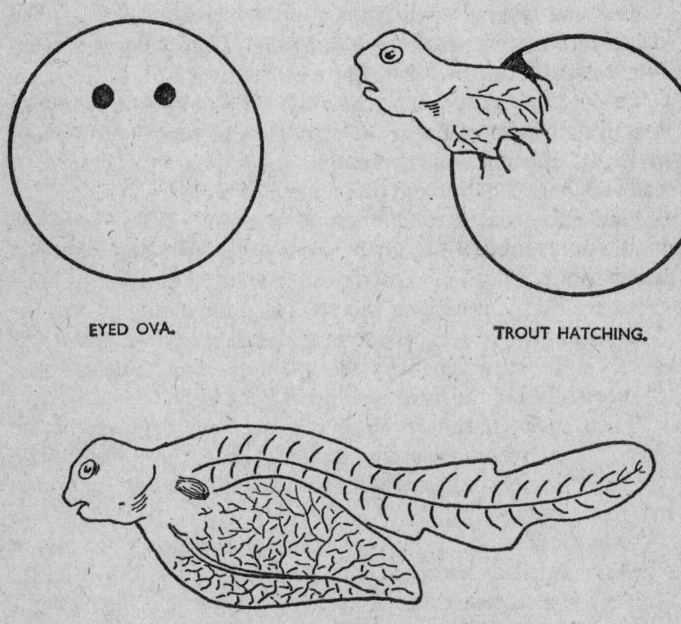

Fig. 1 Birth of a Trout

at the mercy of every creature in the stream, from the larvae of large flies and beetles to minnows and other fish.

From its abdomen hangs what is termed the yolk-sac and it is from this that it obtains nourishment. In a few weeks the yolk is absorbed and about six months after hatching it has the shape of a fish, but with a large head out of all proportion to the rest of the body. The trout has now reached the fry stage.

Always ravenously hungry, they feed throughout the whole summer and autumn growing rapidly if an abundance of food – daphnia in particular – is available. Twelve months after hatching another stage has been reached and they are then called yearlings. The average size of a yearling is four inches, but I have known them to reach six inches in some waters where good feeding has been combined with plenty of cover during the winter.

In some waters, with little cover to break the frost, the death rate among yearlings is very high from what is termed "winter-kill", the formation of ice on the river bed.

In the first two years of their life the young trout grow in length and then, in the third year, they commence to put on weight. Dependent on the weather and food, a third year trout can vary between four and six ounces in weight.

Having rented a stretch of trout water for years, I have had ample opportunity of studying trout in the wild state and can say without hesitation that two of the greatest enemies of baby trout are firstly, minnows and secondly, the larvae of dragon-flies. Minnows are excellent food for large trout, but their worth is far outweighed by the toll they exact. The old rule of the survival of the fittest applies in this case.

Then again, if the gravel is too large the eggs are at the mercy of everything roaming around, while if it is just a little too fine the eggs are smothered. The death rate among young trout is exceedingly high.

Colourations in trout are many and varied. The Loch Leven trout is an example with its silvery sides, but in Loch Leven, the accepted home of this fish, there are caught occasionally trout that are marked with brilliant red spots, and are much deeper in build at the shoulders than the Loch Leven trout. The ferox trout of the deep Scottish lochs and

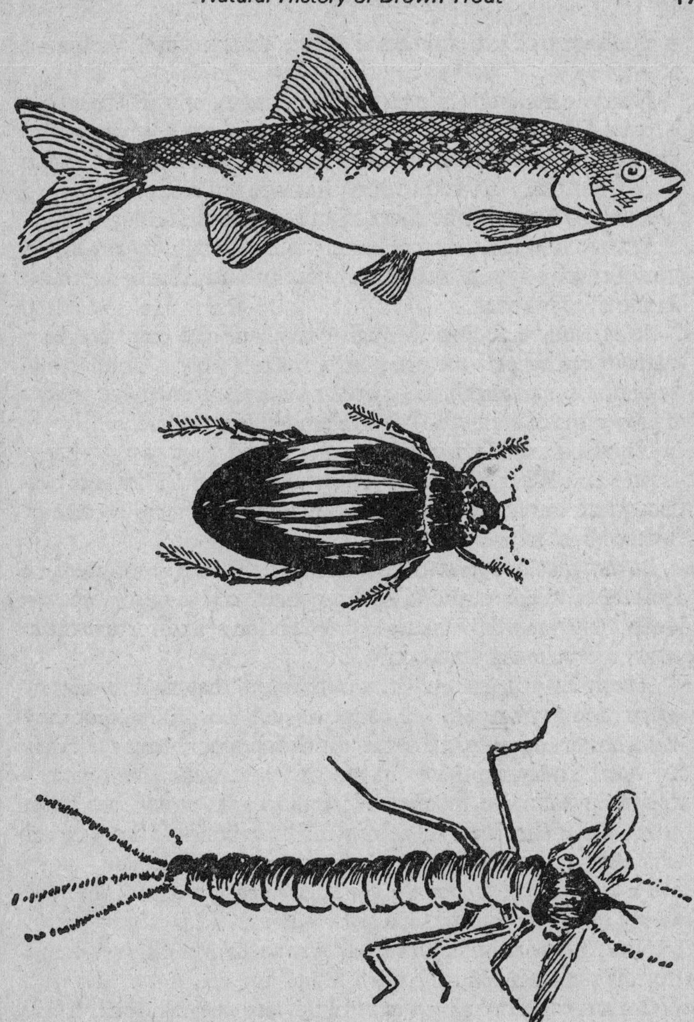

Fig. 2 Enemies of Young Trout
Above: Minnow
Middle: Water Beetle
Bottom: Dragonfly larva killing young trout

the gillaroo of the Irish lakes are other varieties of the common trout.

Many years ago, while fishing the estuary of the River Urr, Scotland, I saw yet another variety when my son caught an eight inch trout in tidal water, the back and sides of which were beautifully marked with red, orange and black spots.

The secretary of the local angling association, Mr. Forbes Strachan, told me that this variety is frequently caught in the very brackish water, but he had never heard of it being taken in the river proper.

In streams that flow through peaty land the trout are very dark in colour and are often referred to as black trout, while in those waters that have gravelly beds the trout have yellow flanks with red spots and are often called yellow trout.

The Coquet (Northumberland) is noted for its large yellow trout. The Rivers Derwent (Durham) and Till (Northumberland) also hold a good head of yellow trout, but they do not run so large as those of the Coquet.

In practically every locality in the British Isles there is a difference in colouration. In those areas where the waters are deep the trout will be black-spotted and in shallower rivers the trout will be mainly red-spotted.

About fifty years ago it was thought that these varieties were different species, but today science has proved that they have all sprung from our old friend the common trout.

After spawning, the trout are thin and weak and retire to the deep water to recuperate. A mild winter will see them in excellent condition by the end of March, but if the weather has been intensely cold for long periods, with ice and snow, they take much longer to get their strength back, due, no doubt, to the scarcity of food.

Some associations open their waters in March, but I feel that in the interests of both fish and anglers, it would be far better to retard opening day until the last week in April. A late spawned fish is rarely in condition before that period and on the hook is practically lifeless, coming to the net without a struggle. A partly recovered fish will grab at anything that looks like a meal, hunger having pushed into the background its natural caution.

In heavily fished waters recourse has to be taken to artificial re-stocking to replenish the inroads made by anglers. Fish propagation is of such importance that I have devoted a chapter to it.

3

HABITS OF BROWN TROUT

The angler who is conversant with the habits of the fish he seeks will always have better sport than the man who just casts his offering anywhere in the hope of a strike.

Three things limit all manner of life and trout are no exception. They are first and foremost food, secondly shelter, and thirdly reproduction.

The main diet of trout is insect life in one form or another. I have caught quite a few trout in my time, and with very few exceptions the stomach-contents were mainly flies and other insects. Granted for the really big fellows that inhabit lakes the bait is usually minnow or artificials like spoons or devons, but even so in Ireland some of the largest trout taken each year are lured by a natural insect – the Mayfly.

I remember taking an eight-pound trout from a Scottish lock on a trolled minnow and was surprised to find the stomach filled with larvae and flies.

Therefore the first thing an angler has to do on any river he proposes to fish is to locate the best food-producing areas, for throughout the whole season those places will provide the tenants for the creel.

Most insects are hatched on the bed of the stream, and those places where there is an abundance of gravel, with a patch of mud here and there, are the greatest producers of insects.

The movement of water over gravel produces a high oxygen content, and in such weeds flourish and provide a larder as well as a shelter for the trout against their enemies. Insect larvae require plenty of healthy water plants in the stream, while bushes and trees in the vicinity of weeds are essential, as they form a harbour for many species of flies in the final stages of their existence.

Good-sized trout always take up residence, in places where

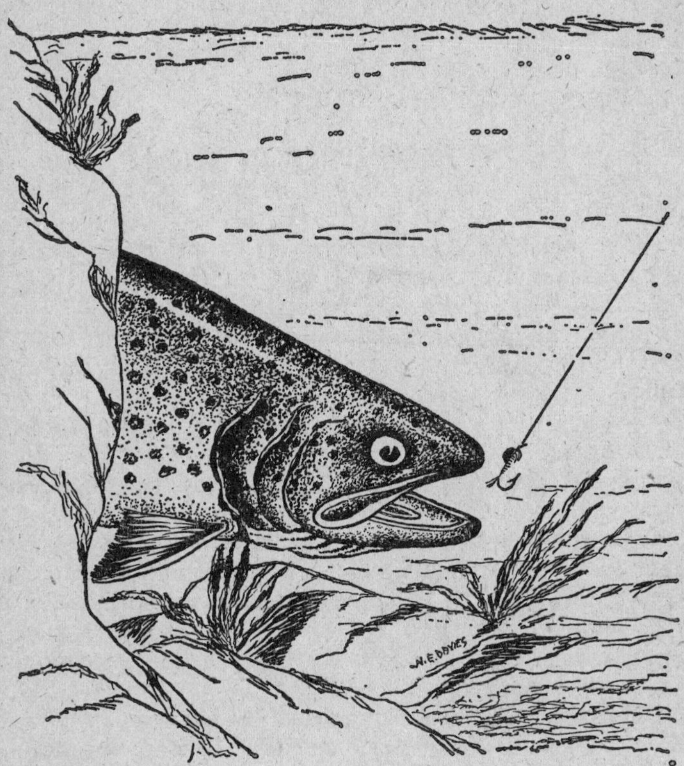

Fig. 3 Brown Trout

they can procure food within easy reach of shelter. Large open stretches of water will invariably be tenanted by immature fish. Again large and agile fish will take up an abode at the side and edges of fast water, knowing from experience that food is swept out to the sides by the current and when a tasty morsel comes along they dash out from their hide, usually a rock or other obstruction, for it, and back again to digest whatever the water has handed to them. Small trout are not strong enough to face the power of pent-up water and so remain at the tails of the more turbulent places. The largest

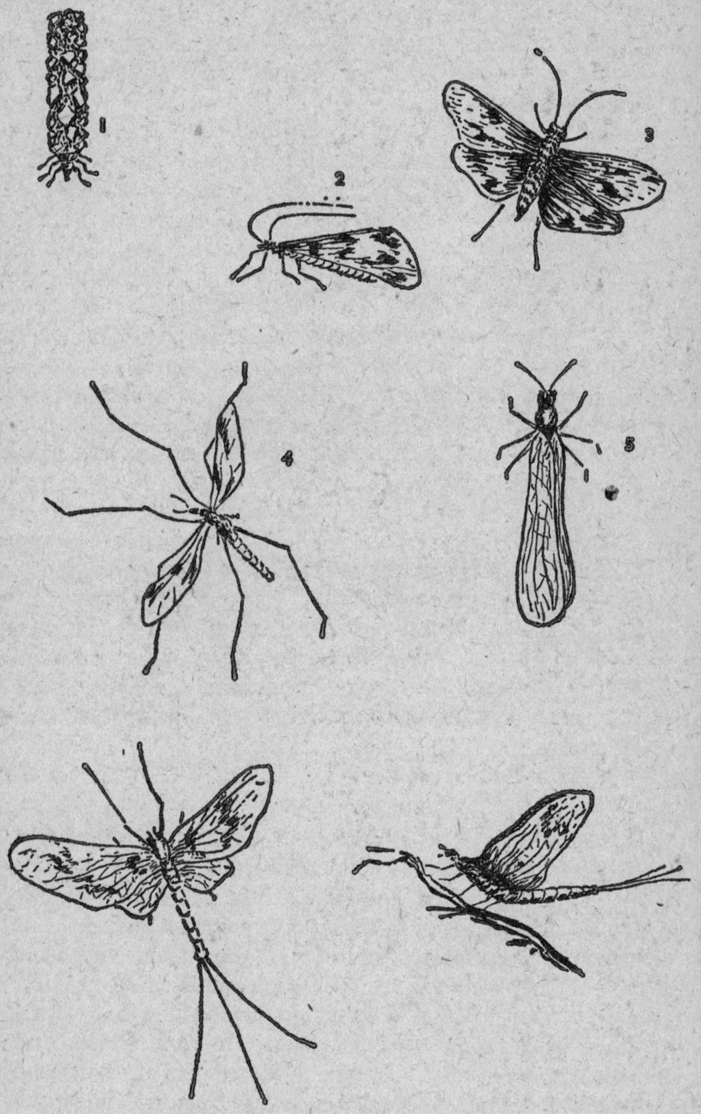
1
2
3
4
5

trout in a given stretch is always in a most difficult place to fish. He has grown large through that greatest of all teachers – experience of the dangers around him – and the angler who would outwit such a fish has to be smart and know most of the answers.

The bigger a trout gets the more prone he is to select those places that are perpetually in shadow; brown trout in particular are addicted to this, making their homes under tree roots and holes under banks. Loch Leven trout, being essentially lake fish, prefer more open water and will feed, when conditions are right, through the day. Browns, on the other hand, much prefer late evening and night for foraging.

In my experience brown trout prefer larger flies than do Loch Leven and the angler who is after the king of a stream should bear this in mind. On Loch Leven, home of this aristocrat of the trout tribe, the locals use, in the main, flies dressed on No. 14 and 16 hooks. One angler I know, who used to fish for Scotland in the International, used flies dressed on No. 18s.

Another characteristic of the Loch Leven is that he shows a decided preference for artificial flies that have plenty of colour in them, whereas the brown trout likes more sombre-hued creations. Of course there are exceptions. We are dealing with living creatures who have their own whims and fancies, but by and large the angler who follows the simple rule of colour for Loch Levens and drabness for browns will not go far wrong.

Regarding rainbows, they can be summed up in one word "Wanderers". Even so, they have to eat and wherever there is a possibility of a plenteous supply there you will find the rainbow. They are pugnacious, and I have often seen them

---

Fig. 4 Some Insects Trout Love

Above: 1. Caddis grub, in case
2. Caddis fly, at rest
3. Caddis fly, on wing
4. Crane fly (Daddy-longlegs)
5. Stonefly

Below left: Mayfly

Below right: Mayfly at rest

Fig. 5 Haunts of Big Trout

drive brown and Loch Leven trout out of good feeding spots. However, one thing to bear in mind, no matter what type of water you are fishing, is that in those places where there is a superabundance of oxygen, there you will find them.

4

TROUT AND THE WEATHER

Weather overshadows most other factors in trout fishing. At least that is what most of us believe at the commencement of our careers.

I was told very early on that trout would not feed in a thunderstorm or when it was snowing, and it was a sheer waste of time to put the rod up when mist was on the water, etc.

All these armchair book theories have no foundation in fact.

Firstly, a trout like any other fish, has to eat to live. Granted his digestive organs are slowed down with any sudden change of temperature, but eat he must.

I have taken trout in thunderstorms, snowstorms, indeed in all kinds of inclement weather. However, do not misunderstand me, for there have been occasions when everything appeared to be in harmony and I have failed, when others were successful. That does not mean that the fish where I fished were off the feed. What it indicates is that another problem was presented and I was unable to find a solution.

The importance of weather in luring trout has been much over-rated. It is nice to fish when the waters are caressed by a gentle spring, summer or autumn breeze and the trout are rising, covering the surface with rings and dimples, or going "mad" during a Mayfly hatch. Most of us have experienced such days, but do they loom as large in memory as, say, an occasion when, with everything in opposition, a brace of good trout were taken, and a problem answered once and for all?

I will concede this, that during sharp changes in temperature fish are not likely to feed on the surface, but they can, and have been taken with well-sunk flies, nymphs and natural bait. The question, and it is not an easy one, the angler has to answer is what are they feeding on? Find that out and you are on the way to success. You may experiment for hours and even days before you discover it, or it may be that the solution will evade you.

In trout fishing faith is a great thing and if we have confidence to face up to waterside problems as they arise, it is odds on that we shall end up by taking a fish, maybe a couple.

Frequently I am asked, "What is the best weather?" For fly-fishing the temperature should be rising, mild weather, or to put it in a few words, if you want a good day go after the trout when nature is on her best behaviour. The extra oxygen in the atmosphere makes a human feel on top of the world and the same applies to the trout. The insect tribes feel this quickening pulse and start hatching and the fish begin to rise.

To sum up: go fishing whenever the urge takes you, irrespective of what weather it is. We anglers know little or nothing about the feeding habits of trout to lay down hard and fast rules. Fish will eat when they are hungry, but so far as science can tell us they have no fixed meal times, so the obvious answer is to keep trying, no matter what the weather.

5

NATURE'S SIGNPOSTS

To the observant angler Nature has signposts on every stream and he who takes heed profits. The reading of such is only gained after years of study; this chapter is a sort of condensed lesson for the beginner.

It is only fair to say that fishing is a sport which is never fully mastered. About the time we begin to feel we are good, we meet an angler who *really* knows how to fish. By that it is not meant the ability to cast a long line: that is a mechanical process which can be mastered with practice. What it really means is that here is a man who can read a stream fairly accurately and as a result consistently catches fish, when others are bemoaning an empty creel.

Some anglers never seem to learn that being able to read a stream is just as important as using the right kind of tackle at the right time. They go on year after year in the same old way and wonder why it is they don't have better sport.

In streams there are good and bad areas and those anglers who live near the river know the taking places and jealously guard that knowledge. A visitor, however, must find them and if he is able to read a stream his task is made easy in that he fishes those places where he knows fish will be. The old trial and error method, with its loss of valuable time, is thus eliminated. Minus that ability an angler's visit to a new stream or lake is practically doomed to disappointment and so we hear once more that time-worn phrase, "Oh, they were not biting today".

I have little patience with those who return regularly with an empty bag and excuses. The chances are that if they had studied the problem they would have discovered the reason to be something entirely different and with the remedy in their own hands.

Trout love oxygen, and on every stream you will find on investigation places where there are feeder streams and streamlets. Wherever there is fresh and pure water coming into the main flow, there trout will congregate. Instinct tells them that such a place, being healthy, produces the best type of food, insects of all kinds. If such a spot is minus reasonable cover, good fish will only feed there in late evening and under cover of darkness. In pools and streamy waters that have little cover you will find that whilst the six and seven-inchers will feed during the day, the big fellows will wait till evening before they venture from their hides.

It is possible that this habit is largely responsible for that thrill-producing phrase, "It's a good place for an evening rise".

Isolated weed beds that well out from the bank are a sure sign of spring water bubbling up. Such beds are meal tables to trout for all kinds of aquatic insects breed there and minnows love such places, all of course being good trout food.

At times such places are difficult to locate, but once found the angler who uses nymphs on his leader will be well paid for his trouble. In such localities nymphs are a deadly lure throughout the season, irrespective of weather and water conditions.

I have seen trout taken on nymphs in a snow blizzard when glycerine had to be used to prevent the line from freezing to the guides, and also during a heatwave in July with the water gin clear!

Whenever I see a kingfisher gazing into a stream from an overhanging bough, nine times out of ten it indicates a shoal of minnows and where these little fish are, big trout will not be far away. If bait fishing is allowed, a slowly spun minnow during early morning or late evening will invariably produce a good fish or two.

Another pointer in summer is that where the greatest number of swallows and martins are weaving their intricate patterns above the water in search of insect food; there the angler will find the biggest hatches of fly. Nature has equipped these birds with the ability to locate such places.

Where there is erosion of banks, insects and worms are

Fig. 6 Swallow
One of Nature's Signposts

washed into the stream by the action of the water. Upstream worming or the impaling of a beetle on a hook is then indicated. That greatest of all anglers, the heron, loves such a place. A menace on a stream, maybe, but also useful in that he shows the angler likely spots.

A heron fishes most in the early morning and late evening during the heat of the summer. Surely from such an expert we novices could take a tip.

Before starting to fish an unfamiliar water spend at least an hour looking the situation over, then map out your campaign, always remembering that the easy-to-get-at places will have been fished many times.

6

WHICH FLY?

The most perplexing and obscure question in fly-fishing is to know when man started to use artificial flies. The nearest answer is the elastic term, "over two thousand years ago". Be that as it may, the old question of which flies are best is still debated wherever anglers gather, and is likely to remain a "knotty" problem to the end of time.

So far as the actual dressing of flies is concerned, we have progressed little in the last hundred years or so. The old colour patterns that lured trout in the days of Dame Juliana Berners, who is alleged to have written the first treatise on fishing, still hold their own in these, what we like to term "enlightened days". But are we enlightened?

Advanced friends of mine with a talent for statistics tell me that at the rate new patterns are being invented there will soon be forty to fifty thousand to choose from.

Now in over sixty years of fly-fishing I have never met a real expert who had more than a dozen patterns. Many of the best anglers in this country, Canada and the U.S.A. relied on fewer. One or two used only a couple of patterns, but they were dressed in different sizes. At the end of the season these great anglers had invariably taken more fish than others who had encumbered themselves by carting around several boxes of flies.

The angler who is constantly changing his flies reduces his fishing time by at least a quarter. Mind you, I still believe that individual faith in any particular fly has a lot to do with making successful catches.

Why then have we so many patterns to choose from? I tremble to say it, but I believe it is to lure the angler to buy them. It is amazing how a few feathers and tinsel nicely tied up can make the unsuspecting angler "bite". Yet bite he does and so until he sees the "light" he goes on carrying round creations in his fly boxes, which, while looking pretty, are practically useless for the job they are supposed to do.

For years I used to carry several boxes of flies ignoring the advice from my parents. Then one day while fishing a Devonshire stream I came across an old quarryman fishing a stickle (stream). There was a fine hatch of red spinners flitting about and still rising. As I watched him he took three trout one after the other, not monsters, but all over nine inches which is good for a moorland stream.

I tried the red spinner as a nymph, then dry and later as a wet-fly and my take was a couple of seven-inchers which were immediately released.

In answer to my question, "What fly?" he replied, "Just an old March Brown which I use all the season". My beliefs about "true to nature flies" received a jolt. In size it matched the spinners on the water. I had some March Browns on size 14 hooks, the old boy's fly was dressed on a No. 16, just two points difference. After two hours' fishing I failed to take a sizeable fish, yet the quarryman kept rising fish and hooking an occasional "keeper".

On another occasion I was fishing in my own country, Wales – I had three nice trout to show for five hours on the River Llugwy and countless fly changes, when along came an angler whose age could have been anything from 40 to 60. From the stream I had just left he took a ten-incher. My flies were as near exact imitations of the insects on the water as man could get. He was using a leader of two wet spider flies, the point being reddish brown and the dropper grey and black.

His creel was heavy with nine good fish. These two patterns served him the whole season, but he had them dressed in three sizes: 12s, 14s and 16s.

During the next five years I came across numerous similar instances. In each case the colour combinations were the same, red, brown, grey or black, as were the sizes used, and so far as I was concerned the cross-roads of my angling career had been reached, as far as stream fishing with wet and dry flies was concerned.

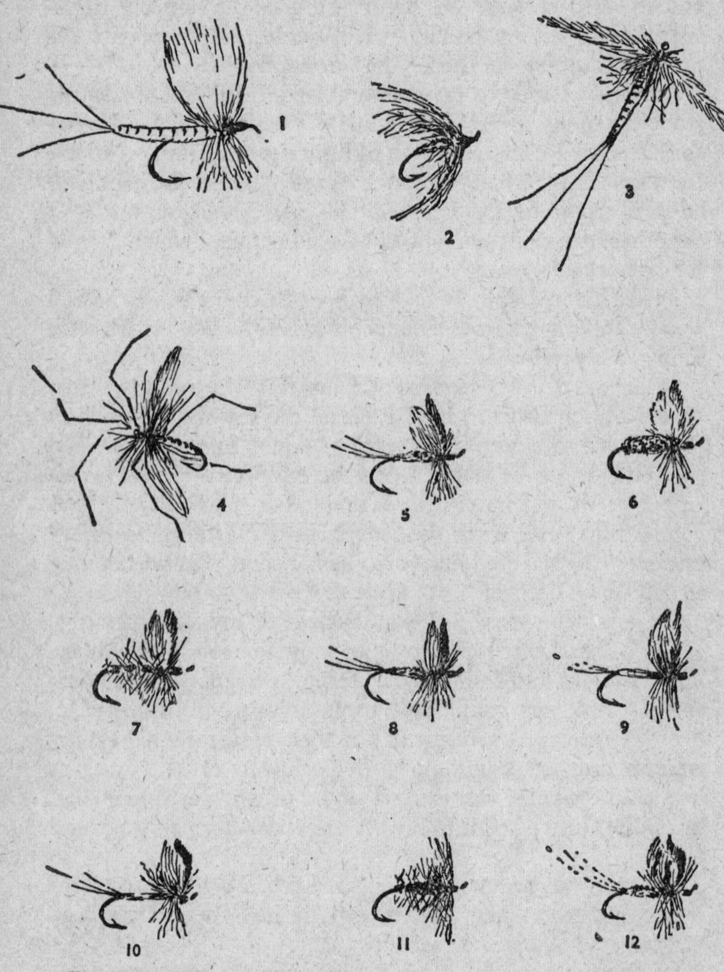

Fig. 7 Mayflies and Dry-Flies

1. Mayfly (Dry)
2. Hackle Mayfly (Wet)
3. Spent Mayfly
4. Crane Fly
5. Blue Dun (Dry)
6. Coachman (Dry)
7. Wickham's Fancy (Dry)
8. Iron Blue Dun (Dry)
9. Red Spinner (Dry)
10. Greenwell's Glory (Dry)
11. Red Palmer
12. Woodcock and Hare's Ear

I cleared out my boxes and was amazed to find over three hundred patterns – some never used. Today my wet-fly box contains 18 flies, but there are only six patterns, being dressed on No. 12, 14, and 16 hooks. The same patterns are in my dry-fly box in three different sizes and for those who are interested, here are the flies I pin my faith to: March Brown, Greenwell's Glory, Iron Blue Dun, Red Spinner, Blue Dun and Black Spider with silver twist. In addition, my wet-fly box contains nymphs of the above flies dressed on No. 18 hooks.

Looking back over the years it is my contention that if anglers matched size and thought less about "true to nature", they would fare better.

Scientists inform us that at best the world of fishes is a hazy world. Objects do not stand out in relief. Light is diffused, shadows are few, and it is not possible to see a great distance. Instead of a limitless sky, the fish has a sharply defined ceiling. Through this it sees the outer world and in it a large part of the underworld is reflected, a grotesque fairyland of strange shapes and unreality.

Fig. 8 Six Good Wet-Flies

1. March Brown (Male)
2. March Brown (Female)
3. Blue Dun
4. Greenwell's Glory
5. Wickham's Fancy
6. Alder

If the size and shape theory is correct when considering the reasons why trout rise to artificials on the surface, then certainly the quality of the "legs" must not be forgotten. Heavy hackle (legs) adds to the opaqueness of a dry-fly and natural flies are almost translucent both as to wings, body and legs. For these reasons I only use the spider type of dry-fly that is sparsely dressed.

When selecting dry-flies, make sure they are dressed on the finest of wire hooks, that the hackle is fairly stiff and that the tail is strong enough in conjunction with the hackle to balance the fly. Many dry-flies today are sold with soft hackles and tails, resulting in their sinking tail first on being cast onto the water. All the grease and flotants on the market will not help in making a badly balanced fly float properly, for the more grease or oil used the more matted will the hackles become. Dust particles will be collected from the "skin" surface of the water and in no time the fly sinks or floats, not as a fly having a semblance of life, but as a bit of debris blown on to the water which the fish ignore.

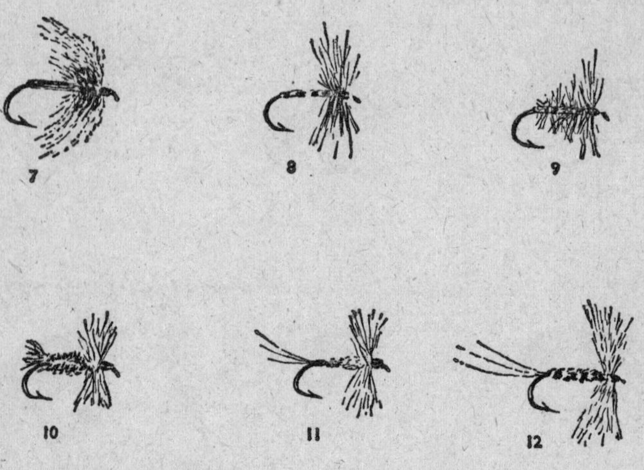

Fig. 9 Six Spider Flies

7. Partridge Yellow
8. Black Spider (Silver Twist)
9. Wickham's Fancy
10. Red Tag
11. Iron Blue Dun
12. March Brown

To extend the argument of sparse hackles. Many anglers have experienced catching a number of good fish on a fly that was badly worn, with very little dressing left. I have on more than one occasion.

If you take a prism to a reflector, and put a sparsely dressed, well balanced dry-fly on the reflector, looking through the prism you get an idea of what the fish sees. The hackle appears to be resting on the surface and the hook is balanced in the

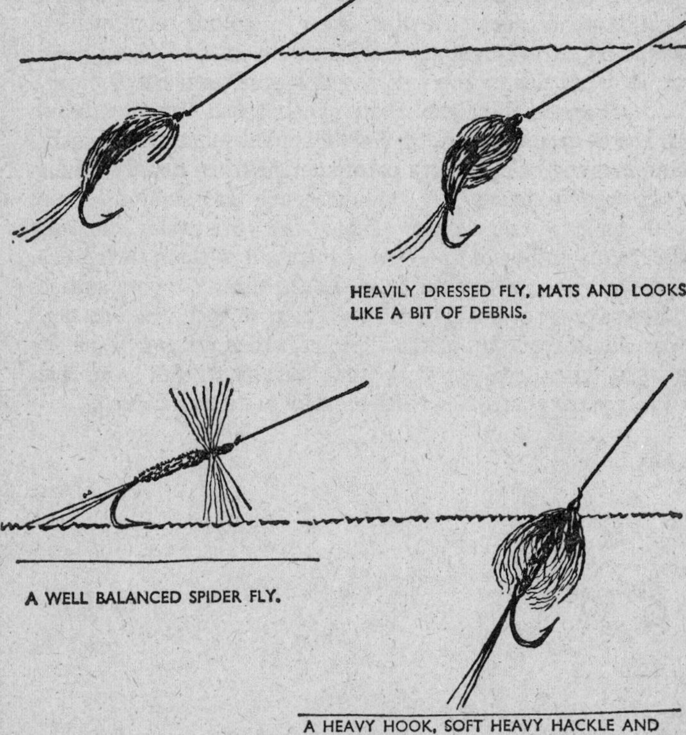

Fig. 10 How to Dress a Fly Correctly

middle by the tail and hackle holding it up. The body of the fly is indistinct and so are the wings if it is a winged pattern.

The scientists also declare that trout in particular can distinguish colours. Maybe they can when trained to do so in an aquarium.

Some years ago I happened to be fishing the River Chess with the agent of the Duke of Bedford who owned the water, during one of the biggest Mayfly rises I have witnessed. The agent, Mr. W. Owen, was a great believer in "true to nature flies" and also that trout could tell colour in insects.

I had been a convert to "match the size" theory for some years then. We had a little bet, just a glass of beer, that he would use artificial Mayflies exact in colour, etc., while I would fish with bright red and blue flies. At the end of the day my take beat his by two fish. My flies were similar in size only.

Until more is known about what a fish can distinguish on the surface of the water I shall abide by "match the size," colour being of secondary consideration when dry-fly fishing.

In wet-fly fishing you get something very similar because you can have a dozen men fishing the same water, all using different flies but of the same size and all of them taking fish.

I remember a day on Loch Leven during a competition. There were four boats with two anglers in each, the flies used were all different but matched in size, and at the end of the day all had taken fish, yet at no time were the boats more than twenty yards apart. Yes, Faith has a lot to do with fishing.

7

USING THE SUNKEN FLY

On opening day the angler who relies on wet-flies, and that includes nymphs, to take a fish or two shows good sense. There are, however, a number of people who say there is less skill in handling a wet-fly than in its dry counterpart. I hate to disagree, but the fact is that it is six of one and half a dozen of the other. Taking a season through, the man who can handle wet-flies properly will always take more fish than the purist dry-fly angler.

Some waters in this country open earlier than others, but a normal spring season usually finds most streams in fair condition for the wet-fly. Look for those bits of water where the current has a tendency to move either over or close to large rocks and boulders, where there is a possibility of a dark hole, for it is here that the really big fellow is likely to have his abode.

The winter floods often alter the lies and feeding places and so the angler has to start searching for them. With water high and often coloured, success will only come to the angler who keeps at it. He must cast hour after hour and never get discouraged, trying those places where experience tells him a trout ought to be lying.

More than once success has attended my efforts after fishing a particular spot from a different angle. But always bear in mind, such tactics do not mean rushing from place to place. Every inch of water must be fished methodically before moving on, and if the rodsman can sense the likely spots it cuts out a good deal of wasted energy.

Where the water is deep and sluggish it is advisable to get the flies well down, and to do this the addition of a "dust" split shot near the end fly will usually do the trick. All really large trout are bottom feeders, for it is there during a greater part of the year that they get most of their food, and it is only when the large and succulent Mayfly appears that they break water. Their principal food is crustaceans, molluscs, nymphs, grubs of various kinds, minnows and the young of their own kind.

In fishing a weighted leader a readjustment of the timing has to be made for on the back-cast, there is a tendency for the cast to whip back sharply and then just as quickly slow up, which means that before the cast starts to fall, the forward cast must be made. With an unweighted leader, should the angler mistime the forward cast he can usually rectify it by giving the rod a little more wrist weight. Not so the weighted leader, if the timing is bad there is nothing one can do, except start the cast again.

Often you will find that opening day fish have a nasty trick of coming short. What causes this, it is impossible to say, but it may be lack of judgement on the part of the fish as to the pace or size of the fly, or perhaps it may suffer from myopia, if that is possible in the fish world. If you change your fly to a smaller one of the same pattern, you will find this more successful.

When you get a strike, make a quick mental analysis of where you got it and why. Was the fly fished "dead" or was any motion imparted to it by the tip of the rod? At what depth did the fish strike? Was the fly moving across the current, or swinging below you at the end of a drift? Was the fish lying in rough water or at the head of a long pool? These are the kind of questions in which your perceptive acumen is brought into play, and the ability to adapt your fishing technique to their answers will determine how heavy your creel will be.

In very coloured or muddy water a black fly will usually get more strikes than any other colour, but fish as slowly as possible, paying particular attention to the quiet lay-byes and little eddies. Remember trout at the beginning of a season are still far from robust for their recovery from spawning is slow.

The strike of a large trout, say one of a pound, is vicious and it has its effect upon most people that are of a composed nature, but the quicker you can control your excited nerves, the better chance you will have of landing your fish. By clamping down on your reel and "freezing", the fish is given an opportunity to break away on a line held too taut. Many casts, and sometimes rods, are broken as a result of the fisherman "freezing". The antics or the size of the fish are not responsible, for a rod that is held lightly and a line that is taut, but not too tight, usually holds the most active fish.

Even today after all these years I get excited when a large trout hits and I am not ashamed to admit it, that is one of the greatest thrills in fishing, for you never know when the really big fellow will come along. When he does, remember, let him have line and go for a good run. It will probably be his last swim, so let him have a good one; it will reduce the playing time considerably.

Perhaps the most dangerous time for the angler is when the fish is coming in, because as soon as he sees you, he will go off in a mad rush and if you are not prepared, it's good-bye fish. If he catches you napping he will show you that he has more brains than you have.

When you have played your fish up to the top and its tail is showing half out of the water, dip the net in and bring the fish over it, lifting the net at the precise moment the fish is over. More trout are lost through bad netting tactics than anything else.

Whenever possible you should get below a good trout after you have hooked it. By doing this the fish is fighting the stream as well as you and its breathing is severely taxed, so much so that the fish is practically dead from suffocation when netted.

As to tackle, the rod can be of split-cane, glass fibre, hollow or solid, or graphite. The last named is a new material claimed to be superior to the other two. It also costs much more than the others. The rod I use most of all is a Garcia hollow glass of 8½ feet in length and is less than four ounces in weight. When purchasing a new rod select one that you can use all day without fatigue, particularly if you have weak wrists, for fly-fishing is all wrist work.

As to the line, a double-tapered one will help in making long casts, but there are other types of lines; some are created to sink slowly, others very fast. There are also lines that float without having to bother dressing them. Such a line is essential when using a dry-fly.

The reel should balance the rod. It should not feel like a large lead weight dragging the wrist down. It should be able to hold a thirty yard line with forty yards of backing (fine line) which is spliced to the fly line. In trout streams where salmon and sea trout run it is not an uncommon occurrence for an angler after trout to hook a salmon or sea trout and then the backing comes in very handy.

Tapered leaders should be used at all times. They assist in casting and nylon is cheap enough these days for an angler to make up his own. For moorland streams the taper I use is one yard of four pound nylon, one of two pound and one of half a pound. Each length is connected with the barrel knot.

For river fishing, where it is known there are big trout, the taper is six pound, four pound and two pound. If it is a salmon and sea trout water the last two yards are four pound. While such a cast is strong enough with a little to spare for sea trout, it is on the light side for salmon, but the angler who has plenty of line on his reel can control his nerves and has plenty of room to move up and down the bank, will defeat even this great warrior.

In Scotland the general practice is to fish three flies to a leader, and when loch fishing it is not unusual to see an angler using four. However, my preference is for two flies, no matter whether it be stream or lake, and if I am fishing late in the evening there is only one fly on my cast. The more flies the more chances of getting snagged on underwater obstructions. Also, when you have a fighting fish, rushing hither and thither, the fewer hooks the better.

I remember fishing a three fly leader on Loch Naver, the alleged home of a monster. There was a good rise on and my wife and I had nine good trout in the creel. As I was lifting the cast from the water there was a boil and the reel whined in protest. The battle, however, was of short duration. My trout line vanished through the guides to be followed by several yards of backing, when up in the air went a salmon returning to the loch in a flurry of foam. The fish fought deep as I ran first one way and then the other in my efforts to recover line. Then disaster. I could feel the fish tugging and I fed line thinking he had gone round some obstruction, but it just lay slack on the water. Another jerk and the salmon was free. But not the line. A few tugs and it came away. The point fly hook was straightened out and the second dropper had the hook broken at the bend. Which hook had held the salmon? I don't know, but it is certain that one had snagged something otherwise I feel we should have landed that fish which looked about eight or ten pounds.

That incident more than anything convinced me of the dangers attending the use of too many droppers. It also emphasised the latent strength to be found in even four pound nylon monofilament.

In purchasing wet-flies examine the hook carefully for on some you will find that the barb is well away from the point. Flies dressed on such hooks leave much to be desired. The nearer the barb is to the point the better chance you have of hooking your fish. The term "pricked fish" arose in the first place through fish being hooked and then breaking loose after a few seconds. A "pricked fish" in a stream or pool alarms other fish and very often "puts them down" for some time, therefore it pays to examine each and every fly you buy.

Another thing to look for is the kind of hook the fly is dressed on, for some have greater "bite" than others. My preference has always been for hooks with a round bend. When you hook a fish the strain is distributed over the whole bend and not in one particular spot, which is the case with some hooks. The barb on a round bend hook, with few exceptions, is very near the point.

While on this question of hooks let us look at it more closely, The hook is a small and humble piece of tackle and yet it is among the most important in your kit. But how many anglers devote the same attention to their hooks as to their rods?

For instance, I have seen flies in an expensive case, the hooks of which had tell-tale dark patches denoting rust. If flies are returned to the case wet, the hook, although bronzed, will eventually rust, and what is more will affect others.The bronze sheath is only a few thousandths of an inch in thickness and once fractured the life of the hook is endangered.

Rocks are very often blamed for breaking barbs and points, but invariably it is rust that is to blame.

A good angler dries a fly before returning it to his box. For this I use amadou, a fungus which likes silver birch or larch for its host. It can be cut off the tree in the summer and dried, and is much more absorbent than blotting paper and lasts for years.

A good idea is to cut a couple of pieces of amadou and glue them to a piece of soft leather so that they will fold together

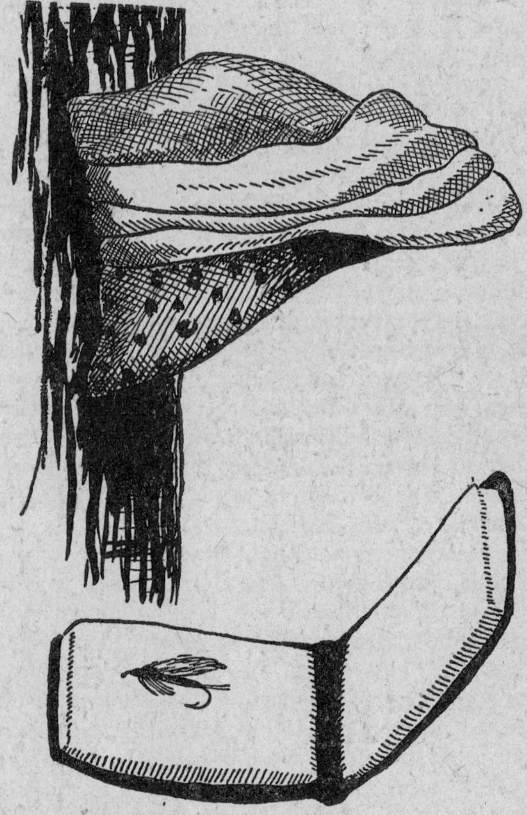

Fig. 11 Amadou Fungus
Above: Amadou Fungus Growing on Tree
Below: Amadou Drying Pad

like a book. You put the fly between the two pieces of amadou, press with the finger and thumb and the job is done, for all moisture is absorbed by the fungus.

Dry fly anglers have been using amadou for years. I have only carried its usefulness a stage further by using it for all kinds of flies and hooks.

A hook suffering from rust is an unknown quantity. It may do the job or it may not. It is odds on that eventually it will break where it is rust-pitted, and usually that happens under strain, like fighting a good fish. A rusty hook can also cause a nasty and painful wound, for no matter how careful one may be, accidents will happen. There is less chance of blood poisoning from a clean hook.

If a hook appears dull at the point the antidote is a good sharpener carried in one's pocket at all times. This may be a fine carborundum stone, a file or a piece of very fine emery cloth. From experience, my preference is the emery cloth, and I use the very finest which is the grade used by jewellers – the abrasive quality is so fine that it feels smooth to the touch. A file is apt to rust and the stone is easily broken if dropped on rocks or trodden upon. Another point in favour of the emery cloth is that it takes up little room and is cheap.

But why all this advice? Simply because it is just such seemingly minor items which make up hook care that make in turn those "lucky" fishermen who rarely lose fish.

8

LOCH AND LAKE FISHING

Every year more anglers visit Scotland to try their luck on the lochs for which that country is justly famous. It is not easy fishing a loch and a visitor is handicapped if he does not know the "drifts" or the strata and bed of the loch bottom. However, I have visited Scotland dozens of times and on each occasion when I have been on a new water the locals have assisted me with good advice. Without such help one can experiment for a long time before the right spots are located.

Fig. 12 Scottish Loch Trout

On some lochs the angler may be fortunate in arriving when a "rise" is on, then it is just a question of the right size of fly.

Some places are fairly easy to read. Flat rock shoals or rocky shores where the waters drop off into deep holes are always good for a cast or two, particularly early morning and late evening. Always seek places when shore fishing where a boulder formation of rock reaches well out into the loch. The deeper waters are always darker in colour, while shallow waters are a light brown or greyish hue generally. A reef surrounded by deep water is good for a fish or two. The larger fish will be taken from the deep water and the flies will have to be got well down, but good sport will always be had among the small fish that delight to roam in the shallower waters around such a reef.

In Scotland there are mountain lochs which rarely see an angler. I know several in Ross-shire and Sutherland. They are usually un-named on the map and the way to locate them is by contact with local residents. These off-the-beaten-track waters are well worth fishing. The fish are not educated and it takes a bad cast to put them down.

For this fishing, brighter coloured flies are the general rule, but if a "hatch" comes on it is only necessary to match the size. The rod for shore fishing and tackle generally is the same as that used for river trout. On the more famous lochs such as Loch Leven, Loch Maree and Loch Lomond anglers are well catered for with boats, and for my part there is nothing quite like a day afloat during May or June, which are usually the two best months for loch fishing.

For boat work the rod should be ten feet with plenty of backbone, capable of handling long casts and also the strain set up when trolling.

In fishing from a boat it pays to engage a qualified boatman and angler, for such a man knows every rock, hole and drift, and if one particular spot does not produce there are always others that he knows of, places that would be passed by the uninitiated. Trolling, however, in all its forms is largely a question of luck, but you increase your chances of success if your lures are working in recognised fish haunts.

One of the secrets in loch fishing is to get the flies well down.

Trout love oxygen and a breeze is a great asset, but good baskets can often be made in a dead calm by light casting, letting the flies sink and then working them evenly and slowly, with now and then a slight jerk. Be guided by your boatman, he knows the water and it is a feather in his hat and also an advertisement if his client gets the most fish. The boatmen are very competitive in this respect. If you have never fished a loch tell him so, and he will be all the more keen to show you what he knows. Quite a few of these chaps dress their own flies and while in many instances they are very crude, they do catch fish, and after all that is the true test.

There is a large number of loch fly patterns, but the ones I have seen most used are Butcher, Teal and Green, Zulu, Mallard and Claret, March Brown, Peter Ross, Coch-y-Bond-hu, Teal, Blue and Silver, Greenwell's Glory, Woodcock and Yellow and Wickham's Fancy.

In lake fishing the same principles apply as regards the locating of fish and also tackle, but as a general rule it will be found that the flies are a size larger. On some Welsh lakes I have seen fish caught on size eights and tens, but if the angler pins his faith on flies dressed on No. 12s or 14s he will not go far wrong.

Most trout lakes are man-made, in which case there is usually at hand a map of the lake bottom. A study of this will give the seeker after trout a good idea where they will be. Land-drainage outlets are always worth a little prospecting, and underwater springs, with their abundance of oxygen, are the finest places of all. Small fish and all manner of insect life crowd in the vicinity of such spots.

Too often the lake fisher is so anxious to get his tackle up that he omits the most important thing, a quiet study of the water.

In lakes where there is a superabundance of small trout and minnows, a fly (if I might be permitted to call it such) that is worth a trial is the pattern called a lure, demon or terror. It is composed of long strips of feather with plenty of silver tinsel in its make-up and when being worked in the water has the appearance of a small fish. Every year large trout are taken on such flies. The best period of the day to use them, however, is dusk when the big fish are just setting out on a feeding spree. Brown trout are particularly susceptible to its lure.

In America this type of fly is more in evidence on lakes than any other creation of the fly-tyer's art, but in that country such flies are classed under one heading – Streamers.

The streamer fly is always dressed on a long-shanked hook and, with very little practice, are easy to construct. For places where large rainbows are known to exist they can, at times, be quite deadly. My largest rainbow from the lake I sometimes fish was 7½ lbs., and fell to a black streamer.

9

NYMPH FISHING

Of all the methods of taking trout with feather, wool and tinsel, nymph fishing is the latest, having come into prominence between 1880 and 1900 through the studies of G. E. M. Skues. Prior to that it had been practised by a few observant anglers who noticed that often when a wet-fly became little more than a bare hook, trout would strike repeatedly at it. Why? was the question often asked. This sort of thing had been going on for years and those anglers who discovered the secret kept it to themselves. Then along came Skues, and he tore aside for ever the mystery of why trout on certain occasions liked very little dressing on the hooks. Such flies had the appearance of nymphs or larvae of the underwater insects upon which they fed. Skues continued with his studies and it was not long before anglers realised that the artificial nymph had come to stay.

On every type of water that holds trout there are occasions when the place seems alive. The fish do not leap out of the water but just "bulge" the surface. This slight disturbance is caused by feeding fish taking nymphs as they rise preparatory to throwing off the nymphal case and flying away as fully fledged-insects.

Under these conditions it is rare for a trout to take a dry- or even a wet-fly when feeding in this manner.

During the last days of the nymphal stage, these immature insects become restive, they seem to sense the impending change and for three or four days before it happens, they rise from the river-bed, where they have lived for several months, to just beneath the water surface, and then back to the river-bed again. This movement up and down attracts the trout, so, long before a "hatch" shows itself in hundreds of flitting insects, the fish have been feeding hard for some time.

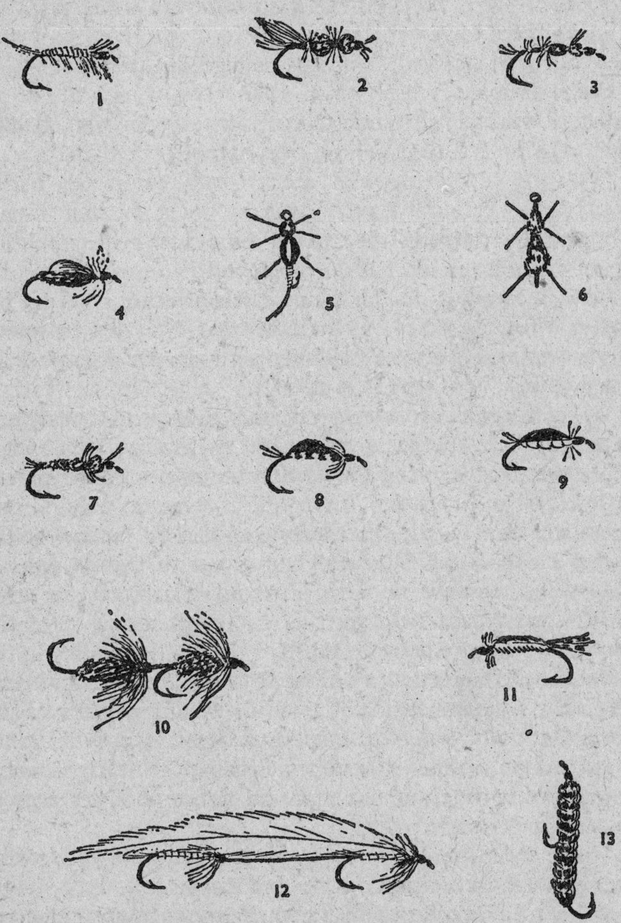

Fig. 13 Nymphs and Other Artificials

1. Freshwater Shrimp
2. Mayfly Nymph
3. March Brown Nymph
4. Iron Blue Dun Nymph
5. } Water Boatmen
6. }
7. Dark Olive Nymph
8. Red Spinner Nymph
9. Blue Dun Nymph
10. Worm Fly
11. Fly Minnow
12. Demon
13. Caterpillar

As the "hatch" tails off the trout return to their respective stations there to rest for some time to digest the food taken. If a cold spell intervenes during this digesting period the trout remain dormant much longer than they would if the air pressure was right. Therefore he is a wise angler who changes over to nymphs as soon as he notices the water "bulging".

With the air pressure high and a steady barometer, I have noticed the period between trout stopping feeding after a nymph rise to starting again has in some cases been a question of minutes, in others half an hour and in some isolated instances, a couple of hours. Immediately after the "hatch" the angler will net a brace or two if he used a dry-fly. However, at the moment we are discussing nymphs and I must leave dry pros and cons to the next chapter.

At the turn of the century certain writers held that nymph fishing was just another name for wet-fly fishing. Granted it is fished wet, but in using the nymph the angler has to know a little bit more about the "insect" he is trying to imitate. It is a waste of time to cast into a stream and let the current do the work, which is what usually happens with wet-fly fishing. Unnatural emotions in the nymph serve to repel the trout rather than attract them, for the "fly" must correspond fairly closely in its movements to those of the natural insects in the water if it is to be effective. If the artificial nymph moves in a way that is unfamiliar to the trout they become alarmed and almost invariably refuse it. For this reason it is essential to use very fine, long terminal tackle which will be as nearly invisible as possible to the trout and at the same time allow the nymph to move freely in the water.

In the majority of cases the nymph must be made to sink immediately. In the old days we used to soak it in water or rub it in mud, then someone hit upon the idea of putting lead or copper wire on the hook shank and the dressing on top. Today for lake or reservoir fishing many nymphs are made this way.

After the cast has been made a second or two should be given for the nymphs (two to a leader) to sink, then the line should be drawn in a couple of feet, another short lapse of time, then another couple of feet should be drawn in and so on until the cast is fished out. This drawing in of the line brings the nymphs up a little in a zig-zag fashion through the water, and as they work towards the angler they start sinking again in much the same way as the natural nymph would.

Cast up stream always, never down. A nymph is not strong enough to battle up stream. Indeed, I have watched a nymph start to rise from a river-bed, but before it reached the surface it had travelled several feet down stream. Those are the motions the angler has to try and copy, the carefree, don't care if I never reach the surface attitude, of the natural nymph.

Nymphs are far more numerous in streams than in pools and they are more active at night than in the day.

In fast water I have had trout take nymphs almost at my feet. The beauty of this phase of angling is that every condition and sort of water can be fished, but the best sport will always be had on the streams where there is plenty of shingle, rocks and bank vegetation.

In every water you have large and small nymphs, depending on the type of flies – therefore it is wise to open the first fish you get and examine the stomach contents. If it shows a majority of small nymphs, match the size, for in general colouring nymphs are much about the same. The same applies if the majority eaten were large. Some nymphs have tails and other appendages, but don't worry about these, just match as near as possible the size. The smaller the nymph the slower it moves in the water.

The Mayfly nymph is nearly the largest the angler has to match, but using the Mayfly nymph is a chancy business until a "hatch" is well underway. Dragonflies are the largest.

Stoneflies, caddis flies and others of various kinds all hatch between March and September, therefore during a dull period it is good to put on a couple of nymphs. Actually, nymphs will take fish throughout the whole season, but unless a "hatch" is imminent they will have to be got down so that they are moving practically free along the river-bed.

When a stream starts to rise after heavy rain is an excellent time for the nymphs, as the greater volume of water dislodges the nymphs from rocks, weeds and shingle and rolls them down stream into the comparative safety of the pools. But not all reach safety, for trout feed heavily on a rising water and the big fellows come nosing up the streams from their hides in the pools, feeding on nymphs all the way.

During August and September a dry-fly and a nymph on the same leader can be fairly deadly, particularly during late evening. The nymph is tied about a yard from the dry-fly and as this goes dancing over the wavelets the nymph, which is on a four inch piece of four X nylon, follows suit by moving up and down in the water. On more than one occasion such a mounted leader has saved the day for me. As soon as the nymph is taken by a fish the dry-fly is pulled under, and although the pressure set up against the fish is next to nothing, it is usually sufficient to drive the hook in over the barb, and the fun begins.

No angler should be without a few nymph patterns because, as I mentioned, fish must eat to live and if they are not feeding in mid-water or on the surface then they must be roaming on the bottom, picking up a tasty bite here and there.

10

DRY-FLY FISHING

In dry-fly fishing you MUST be able to cast a "delicate" fly with accuracy. In using the wet-fly, a fly which thumps the water does not do so much harm as a dry-fly doing so. Wet-flies are early season lures with water often coloured and disturbed by wind and pressure of water being confined in narrow limits. The dry-fly is usually a summer and autumn lure, used when streams are thin and clear, when in fact a bad cast will put all the fish down within yards. Therefore, before the novice graduates to the floating fly he should have had some considerable practise in casting, for often the fly has to be placed in a pocket, inches in diameter.

Most of the fish will be caught by stalking. A good fish rises some yards ahead, but it is useless walking up to an advantageous position: long before the angler is within casting distance the trout has seen him silhouetted in its "window" (the wide area covered by its eyes which science tells us is shaped like a cone). The best way is to creep, hands and knees, taking advantage of any cover, keeping the rod top lowered during the process. A rod-top waving about will scare trout quicker than anything.

When there are no rises the angler must seek his fish, hints on how to do this have already been given. Remember, any spot with reasonable cover and plenty of food is the place for a good fish. Don't cast straight into it, always place the fly at least a yard above where you think a trout may be lying. If the fish rises and you miss him, let your fly continue on well below before lifting it. You now know his hide and you can file it for future reference.

Never flog away at one fish, better have a couple of casts and if there are no takers, sit down for ten minutes or so and look the situation over. Perhaps the fly is not riding right or

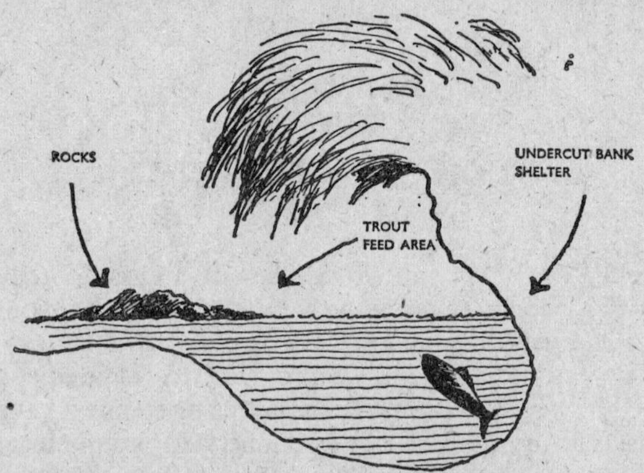

Fig. 14 Example of Trout Feeding Area

it is the wrong pattern or size. Next time try from a different angle.

I remember fishing a pool on the River Urr, Galloway, for a whole afternoon and evening, but I eventually got the fish I was after. Yet during that period my actual fishing time was about two hours. I was at the pool so long that the bailiff came and said someone had reported me as a suspected poacher. We both had a good laugh, but it shows that so intent can one become that time ceases to exist. Of course, any angler would rather catch a difficult fish than half a dozen easy ones.

A tapered line is useful in dry-fly work, as one can make long, effortless casts and in combination with a tapered leader the fly can be made to alight with no more weight than a natural insect. Nylon leaders are admirably suited for dry-fly as they do not water-log so easily as natural gut. The extra elasticity in nylon also acts as a safety valve in that the sudden strike of a good fish is balanced by the stretch. It is amazing what large trout can be killed on even one pound nylon, providing the angler refrains from keeping hold of the reel handle. The handle should only be touched when there is work for it, that of retrieving slack line. Watch the rod top, for it indicates when to use the handle. If the rod is arched it means the strain of pulling off the reel and the weight of

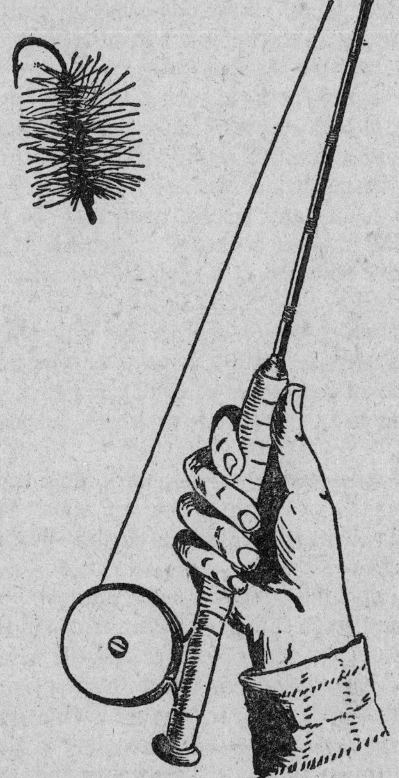

Fig. 15 A Comfortable Grip on the Rod
Above: Large Palmer Fly for Night Fishing

line once it is in the water is sufficient. Time enough to reel-in when the rod starts to regain its normal shape.

The line should be a floating one. Some writers hold that the leader should also be floating, but my experience has been that if the first couple of feet from the fly is greased, that is enough. Ease the fly off the water and it will not be drawn under, pull it off quickly and it will be dragged under and you will then have to dry it thoroughly instead of giving a few false casts.

The amadou "book" already described is nearly an essential when "dry-flying" – the hooks are of such fine wire that if put away damp, rust soon weakens them.

Casting the dry-fly is up-and-across-stream work, never down. Wade as little as possible, for nothing disturbs a stream more than indiscriminate wading. If you have to cross, find a place that creates little disturbance. Remember although you have fished a pool and stream there may be other anglers following, and the heavy waves set up by wading through even 18 -inch deep water will spoil the water for yards behind you.

When a hatch comes on a good idea is to put a nymph on about a yard from the dry-fly. Believe me, you will be amazed at the number of good trout you will get. I am a great believer in the nymph as a trout-getter, whether there are flies on the water or not.

During summer heat trout do most of their feeding between sundown and ten or eleven o'clock at night. Many fish are caught on big night flies shortly after dark during June, July and August.

I would not advise night fishing until you have studied the particular stretch during daylight. You can then pick out the likely spots, the depth of water and the best angles from which to cast. In addition, check over the best spots for landing a good fish. It is too late to think about a landing place when you have a two or three pound fish struggling at the other end. Further, on those waters where salmon and sea trout run, there is always a possibility of one taking your fly. I would go so far as to say there is every chance of it happening, particularly when fishing fairly deep streamy water.

An incident comes to mind when I was trout fishing with a friend on a private stretch of the Tavy. The owner, Mr. J. Tearle, had warned us that in most of the streams there were large sea trout. However, we had seen some fine trout rising so decided to go after them just as the light was fading. We were each using a Red Palmer dressed on a No. 10 hook, with a 3x tapered leader. On his first cast my friend joined issue with something large and after a quarter of an hour landed a six pound sea trout.

Meantime I had lost two fish through snags and had caught a half-pound trout.

We packed up at eleven, each having a nice selection of trout and sea trout. My friend had a couple of duckings, tore his trousers and jacket on barbed wire and I lost a box of flies and casts, which we located the following day. That taught me a lesson. Now when I go late evening or night fishing I wear a special jacket on which all the pockets have buttons. It is so easy when clambering about at night to lose something. Ten to one you discover your loss afterwards and in the endeavour to locate it in bad light you hide it forever by trampling it into the undergrowth.

Always carry a good torch in case you have to negotiate dangerous places. The net should have a four feet cord attached to it, the other end fastened to the bag, so that if you put it down and forget about it, you get a reminder when you feel it dragging behind.

Wading can be dangerous at night on a strange stream. Be cautious and take your time. Feel ahead with one foot, and place it firmly on the bottom before lifting the other. Take the shortest of steps. A long step destroys balance and gives the current a grand opportunity to take hold of the "hind" leg and switch it down stream on the wrong side of the "fore" leg. Such transposing of the nether extremities, is to say the least, upsetting. The feet should be kept farther apart than ordinarily. I always try to face the current.

In choosing unknown streams, select the roughest and whitest water with the large waves, rather than dark water with small ripples. The former indicates shallow water and rocky obstructions; the latter, deep water. It is wise to anticipate a fall and be prepared by having something to hang on to, even though it be a slippery rock.

Remember, deep holes are usually washed out in front of large rocks and other obstructions, and the backwash below such obstructions usually builds up a bar of sand, gravel and debris.

Don't take chances even in the daytime by jumping from one big rock to another, no matter how agile you may be. Many a bad bruise and broken rod have resulted from such foolhardy stunts. The possibility of more serious damage exists.

If fishing a stream which has its source in the mountains, keep careful watch on the water level. There may be no rain where you are but in the mountains it may be pouring and at any time the placid stream can become, in a matter of minutes, a raging torrent, sweeping everything before it. Mountain streams, while providing good sport at night, are fraught with many dangers and forewarned is forearmed.

My son and I were forced to stay out one night in Wales through such a flood. If we had watched the water we should have noticed that it was rising, but the trout were feeding and sport was so good that such mundane things as floods never entered our minds until we both had to jump for it, only to find our return route flooded. The only way left open was by negotiating a ravine. Caution forbade this so we stayed put, partially sheltered by rocks until it was daylight when we managed to scramble back, wet through and hungry, but much the wiser.

Night fishing is packed with thrills, the odds are on the fish every time and when you send your fly or flies out into the darkness you never know what will happen next.

11

UP STREAM WORMING

There are many days during late spring, summer and autumn when conditions are unsuitable for fly-fishing. The water is low, with a brilliant sun revealing every pebble and weed. Using the fly under such conditions is practically useless, so what is next? The answer is worm, but not in the way generally meant. Indeed, presenting the worm in a natural manner takes practice before one becomes adept.

When one mentions the worm for trout the impression is that of a worm impaled on a large round bend hook, a piece of lead on the strong trace, and the whole contraption heaved into a trout hole to await a customer.

I have no doubt that many anglers caught their first trout that way. I, myself, did, and was severely chastised by an irate parent for so doing. But there is another method; one which requires just as much skill as casting the most delicate of dry-flies. I refer to Up stream Worming, the technique of which, I am given to understand, was born in Scotland.

Fishing worm up stream achieves the naturalness of presentation which is necessary to get the best results. An expert up stream worm fisherman will take good trout if they are there, with a better size average than is usual.

Knowing where fish are depends, as I have tried to show in preceding chapters, not upon a sixth sense, but upon common sense.

I learned the hard way. I'm trying to show the easy way. In doing it I'm going to dismiss lake fishing as being too well understood to require specific coverage.

In this type of worming we deal solely with currents and running water whether it be brooks, streams or fully-fledged rivers. Each possesses swift reaches broken up by rocks and boulders, or merely flat, shallow water running over rock or

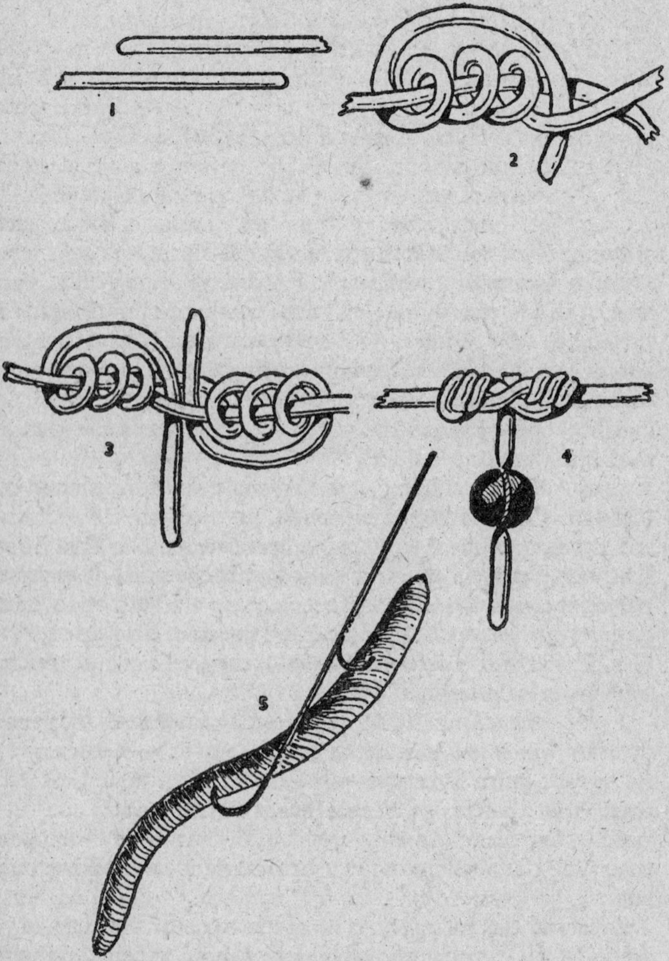

Fig. 16 Knots and Worms

1. Start of Blood Knot
2. The second stage
3. Knot complete
4. The knot tightened up with one end cut off and split shot put on the other.
5. Pennell tackle with worm impaled.

hard gravel bottoms. They also contain pools of varying depths and width, or speed of flow, depending upon the terrain.

Food and self-preservation are the ruling instincts of all fish. This is particularly true of trout, the wariest of the finny tribe, for whether they are hungry or not you will find them close to rocks, fallen trees and anything which gives them a respite from the current, but always within a few inches or feet of where the most water, and consequently the most food, passes their hungry maws, That fact dominates up stream worming, for it is in those places that the angler will get sport.

As to tackle, my preference is for Pennell two-hook, for, with this, I have observed that the trout is invariably hooked in the lip. It is only on rare occasions that I have had trout swallow the bait, as so often happens with a single hook when "lying in". The hooks should be no larger than No. 14. The end hook is fixed near the head of the worm and the second near the middle.

Loops, in worm fishing as in fly-fishing for trout, should be eliminated from the terminal tackle. Loops create air bubbles, add to water resistance and help in other ways to tell the trout that all is not what we would like to have it seem. The hook tackle should be attached to the leader with a blood knot and one end of the knot left hanging after the knot has been drawn tight. On this whisker of nylon it is an easy matter to nip on split-shot if required.

A lot depends on using the correct number of split-shot to fit the place being fished, and frequently it is necessary to change the number several times during a few hours' fishing. Every spot presents its own problem in this respect and this "whisker" is handy as split-shot can be pulled off or nipped on easily. The object is to get the worm right onto the bottom, but not weighed down so it will not roll with the current. The bait should move at exact current speed. Where there is only slight movement shot can be dispensed with, the weight of the worm being enough.

Casting is ordinarily done up and across stream, so that it is possible to get a worm below an under-cut bank which otherwise would be out of reach.

Fast water can be fished with great effectiveness and slow

pools give up their best trophies to the same technique. As the bait rolls towards the angler, all slack must be kept out of the line by drawing in with the free hand, and as many bites will be detected by watching the line closely as will be transmitted by feel.

The hook, or hooks, as the case might be, must be set instantly, and any waiting such as is practised in other methods of worm fishing is invariably a grave mistake.

Pay attention to those places which are difficult of approach and to reach; they are usually the best producers.

Small worms are always best, two inch to three inch being long enough, but they should undergo a toughening process of at least a week before being used. Say you want to go for a weekend's trouting and to be on the safe side want to take some worms along. The plan is to collect them three or four days before and place them in a fairly deep tin three parts filled with clean moss. Each day look them over and remove any that look sick. A sick worm loses its pinkish colour and turns a dirty white. Left in with the others it would soon infect them and the time taken to collect them would have been wasted. Also, a sick worm is soft and soon dies on the hook.

During the toughening period they should be kept in the coolest spot possible, and when needed they will be full of fight. So much so, that it is a good idea to take along a little tin of silver or other sand to dip them in: this assists materially when putting the hooks in. The best breed of worm is the brandling, a pale red worm with yellow rings throughout its entire length, and usually located in old manure heaps.

During drought the task of obtaining worms can be difficult. For years now I have bred my own. Here's how. A wooden box two feet deep, two feet wide and two feet six inches in length is sunk in the most shady spot in the garden, to within six inches of the top. Fill the box to within six inches of the top with rich soil in which a quantity of well-rotted stable manure is mixed. Such a box will support three to four hundred worms. They reproduce plenteously by eggs which are laid in little capsules, the young becoming adult in about four months. They eat earth; that is, they pass it through their bodies, extracting the organic matter.

Fig. 17 Ideal Up Stream Worming Water

In rainy periods the box should be covered to prevent it becoming water-logged, and during particularly hot spells a covering of damp sacking should be placed over it.

The week before you want a supply of worms, cover the earth with two layers of well-moistened sacking and then cover the entire box with another piece of damp cloth or sack. This will bring the worms to the top overnight, where the best can be gathered in a few moments; placed in the toughening tin; they will be fit when needed.

Any worms left over after a day or two on the stream should be returned to the "worm farm" for reconditioning.

At the end of the fishing season, empty the soil out of the box and refill with fresh, putting in your best worms for breeding.

12

CREEPER FISHING

There are times in April and May when the streams appear devoid of fish life. Flies hatch out safely and flit near the surface of the water, for their natural enemy, the trout, is not interested at the moment. He is far too busy gorging himself below, on the creeper.

This larva is one of the most killing baits known, its only drawback being that it is seasonal. However, the trout, by some uncanny means, knows when the creepers are about to make their journey from the river-bed to the banksides, where they emerge as the stonefly.

When creepers are on the move you will rarely catch a good trout on an artificial fly, for the fish are simply not interested in rising for food, which after all, takes a certain amount of energy, when Nature has provided a banquet of fat juicy creepers for them.

The clearer the water the better the creeper will take. It is essentially a stream fishing bait. In a stream the current washes the bait along as if the insect was wandering on its own instead of being impaled on a hook. In a pool it is different, for without movement the bait stays put, and being inert does not attract, for the reason that in all bait fishing it is, as a rule, movement which entices fish to strike at an angler's offering.

The angler must begin at the bottom of a stream, and cautiously work upwards, so as to disturb the water as little as possible. Every cast should be made well up into the stream so that the bait works down to the angler. All slack line should be gathered in the hand. Should the bait stop at any time, the rod should be moved sharply to the side. This will set the hook if it is a trout that has taken hold.

The majority of fish taken on the creeper will be of good size, therefore he is a wise man who prevents the fish from

Fig. 18 Ideal Spot for Creeper Fishing (River Llugwy, Wales)

getting back into the stream, for besides the danger of losing him, there is the fact to be considered that a hooked trout raises a disturbance and it does not take much splashing to spoil a spot for some time. Try to lead a fish down to the quiet water where it can be played out and the net brought into action.

The creeper can be impaled on the hook or tied on with fly-dressing silk. I have used both methods with success, so you can decide for yourself. Number 14 and 16 hooks are the most common in use for this style of fishing.

As to the rod, an ordinary nine foot trout rod will cast well under certain conditions, but my preference is for a twelve foot roach rod where all the action is in the top and middle joints. With such a rod long casts can be made in the same way as when roach fishing. Such casting is ideal for this bait, as the creeper is very fragile and the least jerk will fracture it and dislodge it from the hook.

The fly line *can* be used, but it is not so good with a roach rod, which works better with a fixed spool reel with a line of four pound nylon monofilament. All the weight that is needed is one small split-shot nipped on, two feet from the hook.

A plentiful supply of creeper can be gathered by searching under stones near the edge of the stream. You have to be quick as they scamper for safety as soon as their hide has been discovered. A good idea is to fix some cheesecloth on the inside of the landing-net and then, before you lift the stone, put the net a few inches down stream of it. When disturbed, creepers always make their way down stream and with the net in position you will soon have enough for a day's fishing. These can be kept three or four days in a tin that is filled with damp moss. Half a dozen holes in the lid will provide sufficient ventilation.

The best creepers are those with the pale yellow coloured bellies. They are invariably the biggest and in some Welsh streams I have had them over an inch in length.

Another good bait for trout during "dead" periods is the caddis grub. It is a bait that is easy to find in quiet bends of a stream. The grub is in a little case which is fixed to the underside of a stone or on any sunken debris. On examining the case you will notice the black head of the grub; get hold of this with thumb and finger and gently pull it out.

Use the same tackle as for creepers and the method of presenting and fishing is the same as for the creeper.

Caddis grub can be kept for several days in damp moss provided they are not removed from their cases until needed. This is also a most fragile bait and care must be exercised when casting.

The caddis is a good bait when a stream is dropping after a flood, and is excellent immediately after the "Mayfly carnival".

Unlike the creeper, whose effectiveness is only of a few weeks' duration, the caddis can be used throughout the season. One angler of my acquaintance uses nothing else throughout the entire season and he takes his quota of trout and very often has sport when others fail.

13

USING LIVE INSECTS

Many streams often become low and the waters crystal-clear as the month of August rolls round. Both fly-casters and bait-fishermen now fare poorly, but casting, or dapping, with live insects, including beetles, grasshoppers and "bluebottle" flies, may produce excellent results.

Casting with natural insects is as much an art as casting the dry-fly, but dapping is exceedingly simple along stretches of stream adapted to this form of fishing.

Grasshoppers are deadly lures during periods of low water, when cast up stream, dry-fly fashion, over pools and slow-moving water. The tackle for this form of angling is the same as for dry-fly fishing, although a rod with a wet-fly action is less punishing on the bait. The line should be one that floats, and leaders tapered to two pounds or more depending on the size of fish expected. As to hooks, my friends and I much prefer up-turned eyed ones made of the finest wire, and the sizes should be 14 to 16. Such a fragile bait has enough to do to "work" when impeded by a hook without being weighed down by it.

When streams are very low, trout often congregate in deeper holes, and caution should be used in approaching a pool. Natural insects must be cast with a gentler action than is employed casting a fly, to avoid snapping the bait off the hook. When the insect alights on the surface of the water it usually will float for quite a time, but it is equally effective when submerged.

The cast should be fished out until the bait has floated down close to the angler. While it is floating, the rise can, of course, be seen the same as when dry-fly fishing, but when it is submerged the angler must strike the instant he feels a touch or if he observes a momentary stopping in the movement of line or leader.

Sometimes when trout will not rise to grasshoppers or other insects, they may be brought up by creating an artificial "hatch" on the water being fished. This is done by flipping six or a dozen live insects on to the surface of the water, one at a time. If this does not produce results, it may be found advisable to attach a dust shot to the leader to carry the bait down.

Stream dapping or "dipping" as our forefathers named it, consists merely in switching or lowering the bait on to the surface, the angler keeping out of sight behind bushes, or other natural obstructions. Very little line is used, scarcely more than the leaders. It is not a particularly sporty method, but it does produce results when almost everything else has failed.

Once, on a Welsh stream, I saw a boy of nine take six half-pound trout with a short piece of line and a two-yard length of 2x gut. He lay on an overhanging rock and dapped the grasshoppers on the water. The fish rose with a rush, were hooked and before they had time to flip their tail, were hoisted out.

An insect with which I have taken quite a few trout is the common woodlouse which frequents most gardens in large numbers. In a pool, where there are a number of good fish, toss in one or two first and then cast one impaled on the hook. This insect is very tenacious of life and its attractiveness lies in the fact that its legs dance a sort of jig when on the water, an entertainment trout seem unable to resist.

The common "bluebottle" fly has a similar habit and has accounted for some very large trout.

The hooking of any insect *must* be done with great care or else it will be killed immediately. The hook should be inserted lightly in the back so as to avoid vital organs and if the bait has wings, do not damage the muscles, for a big insect will gyrate and lift off the water for some seconds and it is these antics which lure.

Any type of land beetle is good, and at times I have used wasps when other better baits were not available.

For insect fishing the emphasis is on light tackle.

Live insect fishing is slow work, but it is my contention

that by taking one's time, fishing each spot understandingly, with imagination as well as practicability, one can get much better results than by going about and casting hurriedly here, there, and everywhere. Taking it slowly will always put more fish on the hook; further, it gives a much finer opportunity to observe the essential things of the sport. That in itself, is worthy of the more unhurried and less strenuous efforts that so many anglers with modern and highly efficient tackle nowadays seem to think necessary.

Caterpillars are also excellent baits for fishing holes under trees. Indeed, there are few baits – excepting perhaps the live minnow – with which larger fish are to be taken than the caterpillar, which will be found in considerable numbers on trees and bankside vegetation from the end of July to the end of August.

I remember a day on the Durham Derwent at Shotley Bridge. A deep pool was overhung by several large elm trees. The water was perfectly clear and half a dozen large trout could be seen cruising about. Every now and then they would make a dart at something in the water. This intrigued me so I waited and watched. Sure enough there was a little plop and a caterpillar, still attached to its silken thread, started to sink below the surface of the water. Its progress, however, was sharply arrested as a trout dashed in with open mouth, and there was one less of these ravagers who were present in their thousands and denuding the lower branches of the elms of leaves.

Needless to say, I soon rigged up some tackle and before an hour had passed three of that half dozen trout were in the bag.

Today, whenever I am fishing overhung pools during July and August the caterpillar is always given a try.

The hook should be No. 10 or 12 and it should be inserted in the sixth segment down, just through the loose skin; this will avoid damaging vital organs.

You occasionally get a small trout, but usually when the caterpillars are about the large trout drive the youngsters out of the places where the juicy morsels are falling.

A two-yard leader of two pounds is the ideal strength, and

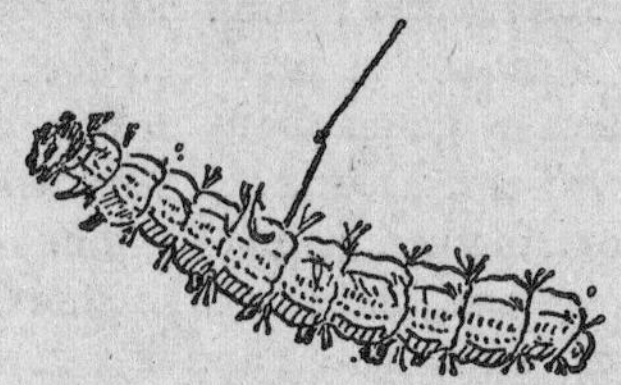

Fig. 19 Overhung Pools are Ideal for Caterpillars
(River Derwent, Durham)

a couple of split shot nipped on 18 inches above the hook is all that is required.

Every available bit of cover should be taken advantage of because some of the best pools are fairly open, so the approach has to be very stealthy. Crawl on hands and knees if necessary –

caterpillar-feeding trout are worth it. Few trout are abstemious enough to resist a caterpillar and several will often be seen shooting off through the clear water, like arrows towards the bait.

Just an instant should be allowed after the bait disappears from sight, or the indescribable, but pleasant sensation which a biting fish sends thrilling through the rod is felt; then strike sharply and you should hook your fish, try and lead him away from the pool without too much commotion so that the net can be used well away from the other fish.

In very overgrown pools one fish will be your lot because you will have to play and net him there. But there will be plenty of other pools with caterpillars dropping in. If you find trees and bushes minus most of their leaves, there you will find caterpillars and you can start again.

14

SPINNING TECHNIQUE

It is well known that trout, in common with many other species, are curious regarding a rapidly moving object which happens to pass within range of their vision and it is this curiosity that leads to so many trout ending up in an angler's creel.

More than once I have compelled a stubborn trout to strike by simply drawing a gold devon through the water so rapidly that it has struck at it before the deception was recognised. Certainly, no natural food ever travelled so fast. While I do not know what goes on in the brain of a fish, I am inclined to the view that a spinner appears to a fish as if something is trying to flee from danger and without much thought the fish attacks and possibly gets caught.

For trout spinning, I prefer a seven foot hollow glass rod. As to the type of reel, there are many on the market today, some good, some not so good, and some definitely bad. For some years now we have had an invasion of American and Japanese reels. After trying some of these imports I still prefer my old Hardy Altex No. 1 for trout. This is a fixed spool reel and is as foolproof as man's ingenuity can make it. The one I have has been in constant use for some decades and is still going strong. I don't want readers to think this is a free puff: far from it. What I am trying to do is give credit to the man who invented it, for whoever he was, to him must go the credit for taking out of spinning a great deal of worry and suspense.

In certain clubs spinning is barred for trout on the grounds that it is not as sportsmanlike as fly-fishing. I cannot see why, with proper spinning tackle, spinning may not be as truly sportsmanlike as fly-fishing even. That one method of fishing is in itself more sportsmanlike than another is a fallacy. Sportsmanship is something finer than tackle, though there is such a thing as "proper" tackle. It is a well known fact that the finer the tackle the better sport results, but it is sheer foolishness to use very low breaking strain lines and traces if the fish run very large. You may land a good fish or two, then again you may get "broken" and the trout get away with yards of line which invariably gets snagged and dooms the trout to a lingering death. For stream spinning a four-pound line is quite heavy enough, and for lake trout you want nothing better than six pounds.

Throughout the British Isles there are spots on most waters where it is impossible to fish a fly or other lure. The answer then is "spin" providing the man with the spinner knows how to handle the rod and efface himself.

If you are a fly-fisher, proceed to forget all you know about that method save the habits of the fish; that knowledge will stand you in good stead, no matter what the tackle in your hand.

When spinning, bear in mind the direction of the wind, and direction of the current, both of which are important; the first, because it is difficult to cast against the wind, the second because the spinner works better against the current. Do not move it through the water as if you were afraid the fish were going to bite; give them plenty of time, and this advice applies more to spinning for trout than for any other fish. More fish are lost through moving the lures too quickly than are gained.

When you cast, give the bait time to sink well down if the water is deep. Then draw in as follows – three or four turns fast, the same number slow, and so on. This imparts a jerky motion to the spinner, and arouses the quarry's interest and curiosity. If you know there is a good fish at a given spot try the fast retrieve process, but when you do this see that the brake is not on too hard, for a good fish striking a tight drum can easily smash the rod or tackle.

It is wrong to assume that force is needed to propel a spinner a long distance. Like fly-fishing, it is a question of timing, and to obtain this is just a question of practice and

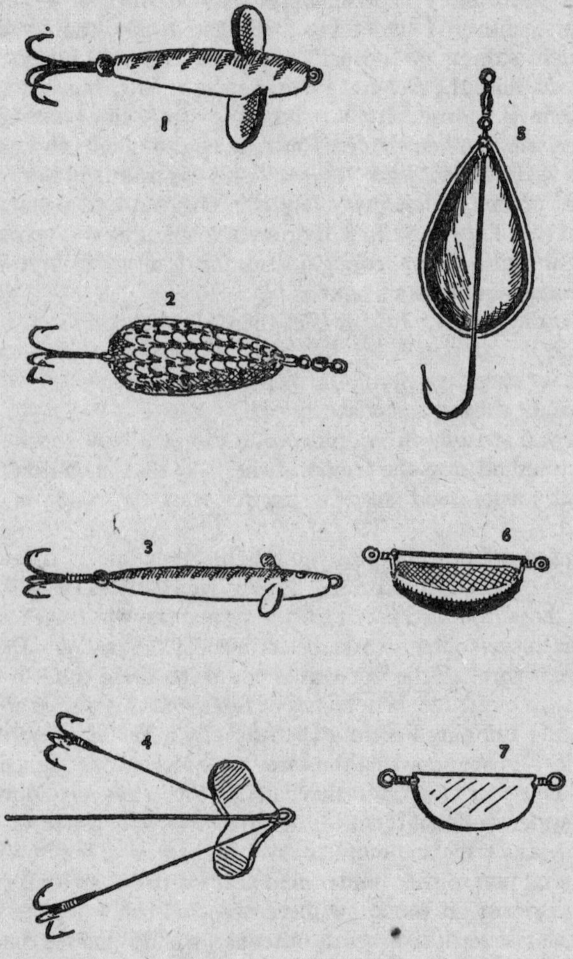

Fig. 20 Spinning Baits

1. Heavy brown and gold Devon for Loch spinning
2. Silver and gold scale-backed spoon
3. Quill Minnow
4. Tackle for Natural Minnow
5. Silver Spoon with long-shanked hook
6. Lead anti-kink for silk or braided nylon lines
7. Celluloid anti-kink for stream work

more practice. A decided degree of skill is necessary in the successful placement and manipulation of a spinner, probably more so than in casting a fly. Learn to suit your spinning to the needs of the particular water fished.

Today the newcomer to the ranks of spin fishermen must be puzzled at the large number of various baits on sale, so perhaps it may not be a bad idea to examine this problem.

In common with flies, there are a number of good and tried spinning baits. Some of the patterns have been in use for centuries and have altered little.

Without a doubt one of the best baits is the spoon, an artificial which has been called on more than one occasion "the maid of all work". It is the oldest artificial bait known, having been in existence ever since fishing began, yet oddly enough there are fewer competent spoon fishermen today than ever before. At least, it would appear so, because a number of tackle-dealer friends of mine have told me that they sell very few spoons nowadays.

However, quite a few old-timers know its worth and year in and year out make good catches of trout with it.

To give some idea of its antiquity, I might mention that shortly before the last war I visited a Naples museum to see some ancient fishing tackle unearthed over the years. There were relics of old flies, bone and ivory hooks and gorge tackles of hard wood and a number of ivory, pearl shell and bone spoons. The age of these baits, I was told, was well over 2,000 years.

For my part, I like the versatility of the spoon, for it can be used with fly rod, spinning rod or short trolling rod.

In trout water it is essentially a big fish bait because, handled properly, it can be made to work close to the bottom where they invariably take up residence. In the deep trout lakes of England, Wales, Scotland and Ireland the spoon has accounted for more large trout than any other artificial.

The spoon's appeal to fish lies in its action, for not only does it spin but it wobbles and weaves an erratic course as the reel handle is turned.

I have many spoons in my collection, but my favourite for trouting is a one inch gold and silver with a scale finish on the gold side. While I referred to a four pound line earlier as being quite heavy enough for stream work, a two pound monofilament line will do where the odd fish may run to a pound.

Cast the spoon up stream and let the current work it down in a large curve, reeling in the slack. When the line straightens out start reeling as previously stated.

A spoon which very often works in lakes is that which is fastened to a long-shanked hook, similar in design to a fly-spoon.

The quill minnow is essentially a stream bait, and being light, is admirably suited for shallow waters.

In coloured water the natural minnow is hard to beat as a bait for large fish. A two inch minnow is the ideal size and the spinning vanes are best if made of celluloid.

With a monofilament line there is little need to worry about kinks. With braided nylon, kinking is an ever present danger, so some method has to be used to overcome it or else it will not be long before the line is ruined. Anti-kinks are the antidote and there are quite a number on the market, usually composed of lead in one shape or another, or celluloid. For deep water work lead is the best, but for shallow spinning there is nothing to beat celluloid or plastic.

A word of advice. When a cast is "fished out" do not snatch the bait from the water; this puts a heavy strain on the tip of the rod. Bring the bait to the surface and ease it quietly up preparatory to making another cast. This is, moreover, sound fishing sense for often trout will follow the bait and take it as it reaches the surface.

Before starting to spin a likely stretch, give the bait a rub over to make it sparkle, for an artificial that glints and flashes as it twists and turns will always attract better than a dull one. It is an obvious thing to do, but quite often anglers overlook the obvious and poor sport results.

In the spin-fisherman's box should be the following baits and accessories: *Devons*, all one inch long. One gold, one gold and silver, and one silver. Two *Quill Minnows*. Three *Spoons*, one silver and gold scaled back, one silver with scaled back and one plain silver, all one inch, and a couple of silver *Long-shanked* hook one inch spoons. Some jeweller's rouge for polishing and some emery cloth for sharpening hooks. In addition, three natural minnow tackles. Anti-kinks if needed. With a box so equipped the angler is ready to fish any stream or lake in these isles.

15

WHICH FLY? WHICH DISTRICT?

In talking of trout flies for a particular County or place, those mentioned include the ones most used by anglers residing there. However, the visiting angler must decide for himself whether to pin his faith on half a dozen old and tried faithfuls or whether to fill his box with individual local patterns. I have my own ideas on the subject as the reader no doubt has realised by now, but Heaven forbid that I should push my beliefs down anyone's throat.

One of the beauties of angling is that everyone of us is free to choose our method of approach, presentation, and the flies we use. It is the most democratic of sports, in that everything concerned with the actual fishing breathes of freedom and it is on that note that the following lists are given.

Among the most famous trout waters in England are the Bristol Water-works reservoirs. *Blagdon* and *Chew*. These waters are stocked regularly with both brown and rainbow trout.

Flies recommended are Invicta, Peter Ross, Butcher, Teal and Red, Teal and Green, Sky Pilot, Devil Dodger, March Brown, Greenwell's Glory and Cairn's Fancy. In addition, the following small salmon flies have also been successful on occasions. Jock Scott, Dusty Miller, Thunder and Lightning, Silver Doctor and Brown Turkey.

Rivalling Blagdon and Chew is, of course, Scotland's *Loch Leven*, where the trout average about a pound. The best period for this loch is May and June.

Patterns in general use are Peter Ross, Cinnamon and Gold, Teal and Green, Teal and Black, Greenwell's Glory, Butcher, Woodcock and Yellow, Iron Blue Dun, Owl, March Brown Spider, Wickham's Fancy, Silver Tip, Kingfisher, Grouse and Claret and Rough Olive.

The above flies are also in common use on the majority of other Scottish lochs.

Lake Vyrnwy (Wales) is another good brown and rainbow trout water. The former average over half a pound and the latter one pound. The heaviest baskets are generally in May, June and September.

Flies used by the locals and regular visitors include Cinnamon and Gold, Teal and Green, Teal and Yellow, Greenwell's Glory, Butcher, Coch-y-Bundhu, Wickham's Fancy, March Brown and Silver, Alexandra, Woodcock and Yellow, Mallard and Orange, Grouse and Claret and Rough Olive.

Flies for Vyrnwy are also useful for other lakes in Wales, but for the mountain lakes more sober patterns are best. Black Spider, Partridge and Yellow, Grouse and Yellow, Iron Blue Dun and Olive Dun are used mostly by the natives. The best time for fishing the mountain lakes of North Wales is August and September.

Good counties for river and small stream fishing in England are:

Devon – Flies in common usage are Pheasant Tail, Wickham's Fancy, Red Spinner, Iron Blue Dun, Greenwell's Glory, Black Spider, March Brown, Coch-y-Bundhu, Partridge and Orange, Coachman, Sedge, and Alder.

Cornwall – Iron Blue Dun, March Brown, Red Spinner, Woodcock and Hare's Ear, Partridge and Yellow, Coch-y-Bundhu, Black Spider, Wilson's Pride, Black Gnat and Silver and Red.

Welsh Border – Iron Blue Dun, Coch-y-Bundhu, Red Spinner, March Brown, Black Spider, Partridge and Yellow, Woodcock and Hare's Ear, Wickham's Fancy, Black Gnat, Coachman, and Alder.

South Wales – Iron Blue Dun, Coch-y-Bundhu, Red Spinner, Wickham's Fancy, Greenwell's Glory, Woodcock and Yellow and Coachman.

Mid-Wales – Red Spinner, March Brown, Black Gnat, Dark Olive, Pale Olive, Partridge and Red, Black Spider, Welshman's Button, both male and female.

North Wales – Welshman's Button (male and female), Coch-y-Bundhu, March Brown, Dark Olive, Brown Ant, Dark

Sedge, Black Gnat, Gold Ribbed Hare's Ear, and Ginger Quill.

Derbyshire – The same as Devon.

Lancashire, Cumbria – March Brown, Red Spinner, Iron Blue Dun, Dark Olive, Pale Olive, Grouse and Claret, Grouse and Orange, Red Tag, Wickham's Fancy, Greenwell's Glory, Knotted Midge, Woodcock and Red Hackle, Black Spider, Tup's Fancy, Hardy's Favourite, Wilson's Pride and Woodcock and Hare's Ear.

Durham and Northumberland – Iron Blue Dun, Wickham's Fancy, Greenwell's Glory, Black Spider, Red Tag, Coachman, Red Spinner, Red Palmer, March Brown (male and female), Woodcock and Hare's Ear, Light Partridge, Dark Partridge, Snipe and Purple, Olive Dun, Pale Olive, Grannon, Sedge and Alder.

Scottish Border – The same as Durham and Northumberland.

The Lowlands – Peter Ross, Butcher, Grouse and Orange. Grouse and Claret, Mallard and Orange, Mallard and Claret, March Brown, Iron Blue Dun, Red Spinner, Blue Zulu, Zulu, Teal and Green, Teal and Red, Kingfisher, Dark Olive, Alexandra and Wickham's Fancy.

Mid-Scotland – Similar to the Lowlands.

Highlands and North Scotland – Peter Ross, Butcher, Teal and Red, Teal and Green, Teal and Yellow, Kingfisher, Silver Tip, Woodcock and Orange, Woodcock and Red, Grouse and Orange, Grouse and Yellow, Heather Fly, Red Spinner and Alexandra.

Ireland – Throughout the whole of this country the patterns used in Great Britain will be found quite acceptable to the Irish trout. Whenever I have visited this angler's paradise my faith has been placed in the half dozen I listed in Chapter 6.

16

RE-STOCKING TROUT STREAMS

For years trout-fishing associations throughout the country have each year released thousands of fry and fingerlings, yet generally speaking fishing is getting poorer every year. As a result, sportsmen are becoming increasingly conscious of the need to limit catches.

In the space of this chapter let us look at the question of natural spawning and artificial stocking. In the first place, most hatchery men I have met say that the spawn of small fish and that from large fish give the same results in the fry produced, while a number of bailiff friends of mine are just as sure that the eggs from large fish produces better and stronger fry.

My observations indicate that both these views are correct in the circumstances under which the observations were made.

One result of fish propagation in a stream is the asking of many questions such as: What becomes of the fish after they have been planted? Is the system of planting correct? Are we planting fish to feed the fish already in the waters?

In this country we have no Government-controlled trout hatcheries. Those that we have are operated for profit and the conditions are designed to save most of the fry hatched, and the food and care they get enable nearly all of them to live and grow. However, the efficiency in hatching fish is greater than that exercised in many cases when re-stocking takes place.

Only a short while ago, I heard of one association dumping – and I mean dumping, 5,000 trout fry into the shallows of a trout stretch. In those waters were predatory minnows by the thousand. I leave you to guess what chance those 5,000 had of survival. And so it goes on year after year, thousands of fry released with little return to the man who pays for it – the angler.

Under the natural conditions things are different. Small fish use small gravel for their spawning beds with the result that only a small percentage of the eggs come to fruition. Floods and current changes sweep the small stones away and the eggs are soon lost. Spawning beds of large trout are on much larger gravel with the result that they are better able to withstand current changes, etc. For this reason alone the percentage of hatch from eggs spawned by large fish is much greater.

With wild fish spawn, natural selection operates from the beginning, and the weak and unfit are weeded out at once, thus only strong and vigorous fish grow up. In a hatchery the weak are made to live where they would perish under natural conditions.

Of course, if an association has a pond or two for fry to grow in, and providing there are no predators present, the results are not too bad.

As to the best time to re-stock, my observations lead me to the belief that the close season is best, for it enables the new fish to get their bearings and learn something about the rigours of primitive life, which is most essential if the angler is to be assured of sport.

Where spawning conditions are good and there is suitable water for small fish to grow in, I am of the firm conviction that the putting in of large spawning fish, if there are not enough left in the stream, will do more than anything else to bring back good fishing to depleted waters.

For fish to grow large, there must be plenty of the right food. On a stretch where there are few bushes and little bank-side vegetation, a good idea is to bundle a number of tree sticks together with wire and let the bundle hang close in to the bankside. As the sticks become waterlogged the bundle will sink and the tethering wire (galvanised is best) should be just long enough to let it rest on the bottom. In the summer these bundles become the home of myriads of insects which will populate the stream.

Mayflies, stoneflies, sedge, etc., can all be transported from one spot to another with the aid of muslin bags.

There is one fly, however, which, although looking very

beautiful on a summer evening as it hovers and hawks over a stream, is deadly to newly hatched trout and that is the dragonfly. The larvae of this insect, if in great numbers, will denude a stream of alevin in very short time and will also play havoc among the insect population, therefore see that the tribe of Libellula (dragonfly) is kept in check.

In some reaches there may be few shelters, but this can be remedied by putting in rocks, tree trunks, etc., and these

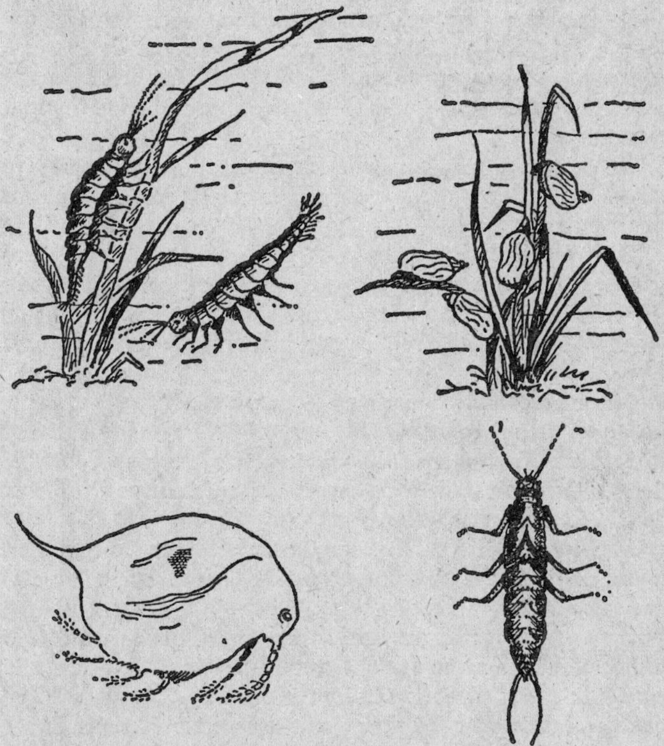

Fig. 21 Underwater Animal Life
Above left: Freshwater Shrimp
Above right: Mollusca
Below left: Daphnia (Water Flea)
Below right: Creeper (Larva of the Stonefly)

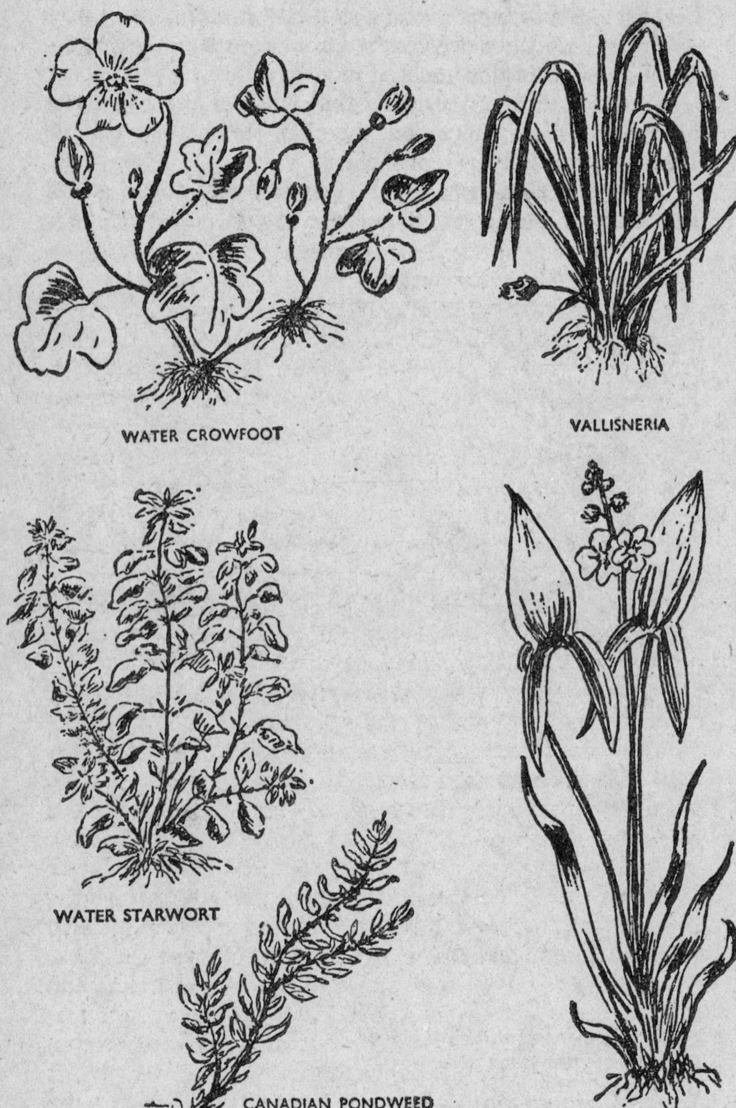

Fig. 22 Good Weeds

artificial aids will serve a dual purpose, for not only will they become shelters, but eventually will become feeding stations by reason of the eddies created.

In quiet pools it is a good investment to put in a number of daphnia (water flea). Actually, it is neither insect nor flea, but a minute freshwater crustacean which young trout love. Its fecundity is extremely high, and once established in a stretch, there is little danger of it dying out. The daphnia has a life-span of ten days; it has but a single eye and reproduces by means of eggs in three days.

Weeds are also of great importance in trout water providing shelter and food and the following trio are the best that can be introduced: celery (*Apium Inundatum*), water starwort (*Callitriche aquatica*), and the water crowfoot (*Ranunculus aquatilis*).

Each will hold a large quantity of insect life; what is more, none is difficult to keep under control. One weed that should never be allowed in a stream or pool is ribbon weed, for it collects mud and in a very short time will have smothered the good weeds and the trout will seek pastures new.

One of the surest ways of conserving a trout population is to increase the size-limit and limit the take. With few exceptions, the size to catch is seven inches. Seven inches is ridiculously low. My viewpoint is that nine inches should be the figure, no matter what type of stream it is, and the catch limit should be fixed by each individual angling body concerned.

In lakes with an abundance of food and cover, trout are much larger, generally speaking, but even so the size limit is very low in many places.

Water improvement is fascinating, but it requires hard work and planning, if the results are to be permanently satisfactory. Some associations are not rich enough to support a qualified bailiff, but I feel sure that if the members of these particular clubs looked upon the close season as one of preparation and the members rolled up their sleeves and got down to the job, their sport in a couple of years would more than compensate for the energy expended. Far too often the hard work is left to a few stalwarts while the main body of the club reap the benefit.

On more than one occasion I have been asked why it is that some waters produce an abundance of pink-fleshed trout other than Loch Leven. The simple answer is that there is a good supply of *Mollusca*, a water snail, and also *Gammarus Pulex*, the common fresh water shrimp. It has been found by experiment that these two items in a trout's diet produces pink-fleshed trout. Both are prolific breeders, and once planted in suitable areas, soon populate the whole stretch. Waters in which it does not occur should be stocked at once.

The Daphnia is essentially a food for young fish. The Creeper, larvae of the Stonefly, is easily collected in May from streamy water and can just as easily be transferred to other sections that are minus this valuable trout food.

If one is considering putting in minnows as food, the subject should be given much thought. Too much bottom food will ultimately result in large fish, but they will not be free risers to the artificial fly. The aim should be to produce free rising fish and that can only be done by planting an abundance of insect food. It is one thing in the trout fishing cycle you cannot overdo.

17

CARE OF TACKLE

Except in very few places September 30 marks the end of the trout season. Even so the angler who takes a pride in his tackle has quite a lot to do if it is to be in first class condition when "opening day" rolls round once more. Make no mistake, if your kit is not properly taken care of during the six months' dormant period it will most certainly let you down when least expected.

In these days of high prices it pays to spend a little time overhauling tackle. It is wrong to leave the hundred and one jobs until the eve of another season because one is liable to scamp them then.

My first task has always been to check every inch of each of my rods. During a season's wear and tear it is amazing what damage can be done, which can only be detected by close examination. Sometimes a whipping becomes frayed, or on a spinning rod, a ring is cracked, in which case it must be renewed. Afterwards, take a close look at the varnish for signs of cracks. If these are left unattended it would allow that arch enemy of all split cane rods, damp, to get in. Once it enters all the varnish in the world will not allay its insidious progress of destruction and in a matter of months the rod is practically useless. If the varnish sheath is not fractured too badly, a spot or two of varnish will do the job. But if in doubt, it is a wise precaution to strip the rod, revarnish and whip. It will take some time as the varnishing is best done during a spell of dry weather. Moisture in the atmosphere tends to keep the varnish tacky for a long period, and during that time it will collect dust and thus spoil the finish when dry. Always use a good grade of varnish.

If there are any doubts in your mind about damp in the segments of the rod, your best move is to send it to a good rod-maker and he will attend to it scientifically, which is beyond the scope of amateurs.

If the rod is in good trim all that is needed is a rub down with some good wax polish similar to that used for parquet flooring.

With fibre-glass rods there is no need to worry about damp, but rings and whippings should be carefully examined. Before storing, they should be given a good rub down with wax. Nowadays such polish can be purchased in pressure spray cans and is much easier to use. Cracks in the varnish may occur anywhere, but seem to develop most where the rod meets the ferrule.

When I am satisfied that each rod is in order they are stored in a dry place where the temperature is fairly even. Never put your rods into any old corner.

My next job is to overhaul the reels. I have always been amazed at the amount of dirt and grit a reel will collect during even a day's usage.

Each reel is taken down and every piece of mechanism is washed in methylated spirits. This gets most of the foreign particles off, then I go over ratchets and pawls with a No. 5 squirrel-hair water-colour paint brush dipped in meths. When satisfied that each part is perfectly clean, the parts are oiled and assembled. Never use cheap oil, and don't drown the parts in oil or when you come to use the reel it will throw oil all over the place.

Fly reels are easy to take down and assemble, but spinning reels take a little time. If each part is placed on a white plate or in a tin there is no danger of their being lost. Believe me, in spinning reels there are a number of very small screws which, should they fall on a rug or carpét, will provide work for the family in locating them. If you should be unfortunate enough to drop a screw, use this method to find it. Get a magnet and go over the area on the rug where it fell.On more than one occasion I have blessed the day I invested a few pence for a magnet.

Fly lines also gather a lot of dirt despite their plastic sheath. My practice is to rub a line down after each day's fishing, and then at the end of the season to give them a wash in rain-water. Each line is then wound on to a line-dryer and stored.

Tapered nylon leaders are easy to make and during a winter's evening a dozen can be prepared easily, using a four-fold knot to connect the lengths of different thickness.

For checking over the contents of fly-boxes and hooks, a good magnifying glass is essential. Examine first the barb of each fly and then the point and lastly the head. In the case of a blunt point a rub with fine emery cloth will do the trick. To examine a No. 18 hook you will find the glass handy. If you have not such a thing as a glass, put the hook on a sheet of white paper and look at it carefully. Any defects in the hook will show up. If the barb has gone put the hook in the fire.

The head of a fly gets considerable wear in use, but a drop of clear nail varnish applied with a sewing needle is good first-aid treatment. In the case of dry-flies a steam bath will, in nine cases out of ten, renew their freshness. Hold the fly with a pair of tweezers in the steam which billows from the spout of a boiling kettle. Five or six seconds for each fly is sufficient.

Lastly, all flies are treated with moth repellent and the best I know is paradichlorate of benzine, which can be purchased in crystal form from most chemists. Reduce the crystals to powder by rolling them with an ordinary lemonade bottle, then sprinkle the powder in the box or between the leaves of the book.

Polish all your artificial baits and when clean, give the hooks a rub over or renew if any show signs of rust or are in any way damaged. Remember, the hook is what connects you to the fish.

It is also a good idea to warm some oil and place all swivels in it for a few minutes and then place them on a sheet of blotting paper to drain and dry. A swivel that does not function is a curse when one is spinning.

To complete your chores, give your waders or rubber thigh boots a good clean, and if a suspected fracture reveals itself, put a patch on. With a self-vulcanizing kit now on sale this is easy and makes a much neater job than the old style of patching.

Clean your creel or bag with soap and water and hang in a dry place. When perfectly dry give the creel a good coat of varnish. If your container is canvas, give it a good washing

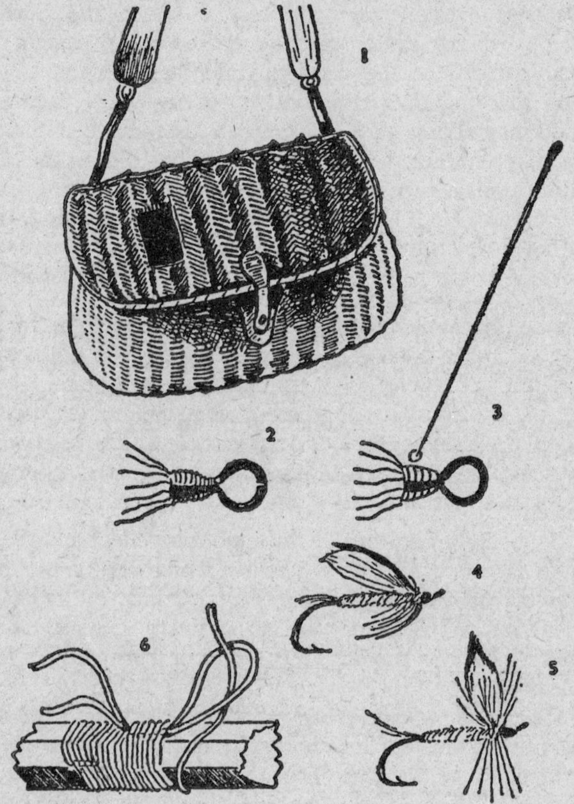

Fig. 23 Winter Chores

1. Creel, cleaned and varnished, hanging up to dry
2. Head of fly before attention
3. After first-aid with nail varnish
4. Bedraggled, winged dry-fly
5. Beauty regained with steam bath
6. Finish off a new whipping

inside and out, for it is amazing how long a fishy smell can last, and the only thing I know for removing it is a good scrub with soap and water.

Well, there you are: for the angler there need never be such things as tiresome winter evenings.

18

THE RAINBOW TROUT

I started trout fishing at the age of seven, which is several decades ago, but it was not until reaching 32 that a rainbow came to my net, and then it was not in this country.

I was at the time employed in New York, U.S.A., when a colleague, whose parents lived in Alaska, near Lake Iliamna, invited me for a fishing holiday in that angling paradise.

We started fishing the lake on the evening of our arrival, and in two hours our joint take was nine rainbows. Two ten pounders were retained for food and the rest were released. Nearly all were taken on streamer flies, dressed on No. 6 long-shanked hooks.

In British Columbia, Canada and various parts of the U.S.A. where I fished it was nearly always the same: the largest fish falling to the lure of a streamer.

In these Isles of ours we have very few streams where one can take a wild rainbow, but we have lakes and reservoirs where they are planted. I am sure that both in Wales and also Scotland there are fast-running waters that would suit them. If planted, who knows, after a few years there may evolve a run of steelhead trout, which are simply rainbows that go to sea and then return to fresh-water to spawn. During my stay in the U.S.A., I caught many steelheads, and pound for pound, they are the equal of a fresh-run salmon in fighting ability.

It was while in British Columbia that I had my first taste of smoked rainbow. Today any angler in the British Isles can smoke his catch of brown or rainbow by simply purchasing a smoking outfit from a tackle shop. The best kind of sawdust to use, no matter what species you want to treat, is oak. Fillet the fish before treatment and, to put it in a few words, smoked trout are delicious.

Fig. 24 Rainbow Trout

But to return, the man after rainbows must bear in mind that a brown trout strikes much more slowly than a rainbow. For instance, a brown trout will very often come up behind the fly and follow it for some distance before he decides to take it. When he does decide, he overtakes the fly, opens his mouth and takes it in.

A rainbow on the other hand, usually takes a fly hard and fast. He hits it from any direction without any hesitation, like a rugby player making a tackle. So to hook a rainbow an angler needs to be more alert, more keyed up and a good deal faster on the strike than for a brown. I say this with all due respect to the latter.

When hooked, a rainbow very often leaves the water in a flashing leap, and in this respect females leave the water more often than males. Another characteristic is that it is more of a bottom feeder, with the result that many flies, including nymphs, are weighted so that they can be worked on or near the bottom. Some rainbows I have caught had their noses rubbed raw, no doubt due to grubbing about among the gravel for nymphs and other kinds of food. For rainbow fishing the wise angler always has a few weighted nymph and fly patterns in his box.

Like other confined water fish, this species is attracted by under water conditions, where abrupt out-croppings provide shade and concealment. Coarse gravel breeds insect life and crustaceans. An under water spring hole is almost a sure bet that there will be a fish or two in the area. A lake bottom bare of cover usually plays host to few fish. Wise anglers watch for the ideal combination of a food-producing bottom with protective hiding spots in the same vicinity. If a particular water is fished often enough it is an easy matter to memorise the producing areas.

When fishing a strange water I make a habit of examining the stomach contents of my first fish and then try to match in colour and size the nymphs or flies it has been enjoying. When a fish's stomach is jammed with insects, dump the lot in a jar of water and shake. This separates insects for identification. Be guided accordingly.

Here now are instructions on how to dress some of the flies

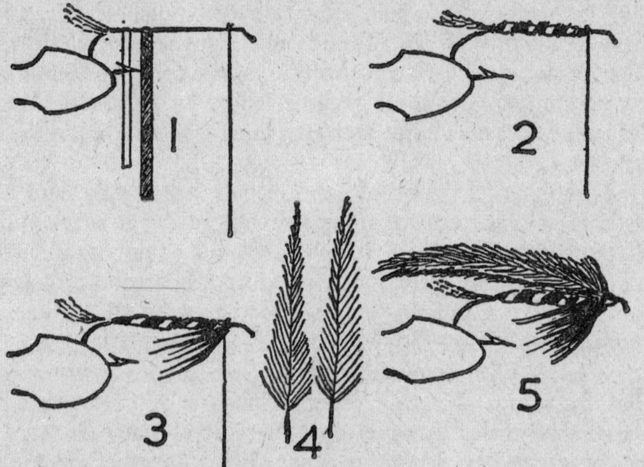

Fig. 25 Dressing the Black Streamer Fly

1. A tail of Golden Pheasant breast feather fibres is tied in, also a length of flat silver tinsel and one of black wool. The tying silk is wound back.
2. Body is complete.
3. A throat hackle of black feather fibres is put on.
4. Two black cock hackles.
5. The cock hackles are put on and a black varnish head completes the streamer.

that have proved their worth for a place on any angler's leader.

First and foremost a streamer fly, and I give the Black Streamer pride of place.

As to nymphs, there are scores of patterns, but one my friends and I are never without is the hatching Olive. Not only is it good for rainbows, but browns seem to like it, particularly during the early part of a season.

My next, what I term "old standby" is the Black and Peacock Beetle. This pattern is also fairly easy to create. All my nymphs for rainbows are dressed on No. 10 hooks, and beetles on No. 8.

If you are going to fish fairly deep water, then by all means

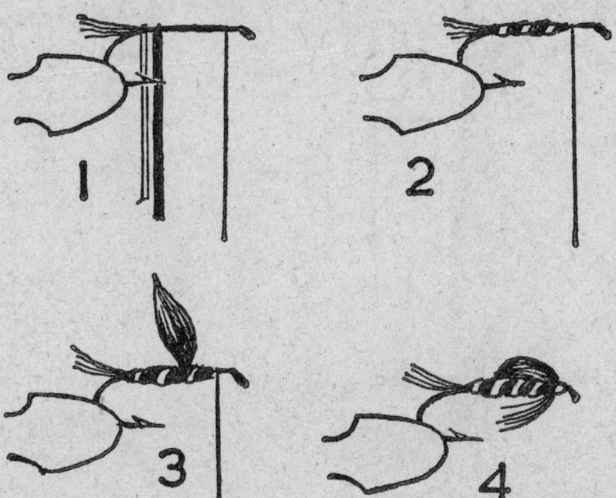

Fig. 26 Hatching Olive Nymph

1. A short tail of olive-coloured hackle feather fibres is tied in, also a length of fine oval silver tinsel and a length of olive wool. The tying silk is wound back to near the eye.
2. The body is complete.
3. A section from an olive-coloured feather is tied in, also a throat hackle of olive fibres.
4. The feather section is brought over and tied in and we have the finished nymph.

give your patterns a foundation of fine lead or copperwire and use a fast sinking line.

Whenever I go lakc or reservoir fishing I take a couple of reels; one is loaded with a floating line and the other with one that sinks. Of course, with some reels you can carry a spare drum.

Of all the patterns that have been invented since the rainbow became all the rage there are three that I can thoroughly recommend: Dambuster, Baby Doll and Sweeny Todd. In each case the hook is No. 8 or No. 10, long-shank.

The first named is a most useful lure throughout the entire season. Here is the dressing: Tail: a small tuft of bright yellow wool. First half of body is bronze peacock herl, then a Rhode Island Red cock hackle is wound in, three turns is

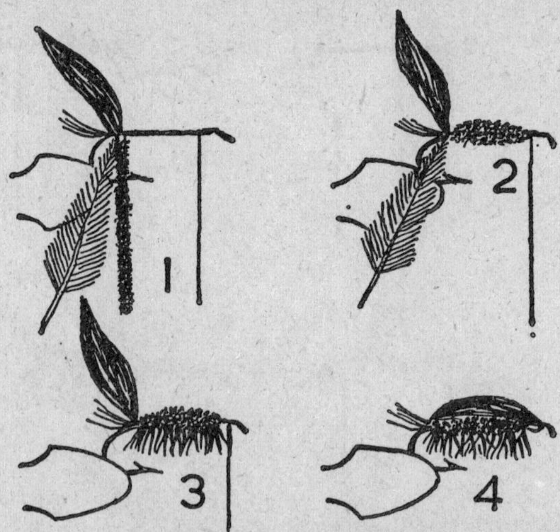

Fig. 27 Dressing the Black and Peacock Beetle

1. A tail of yellow feather fibres is tied in, also a badger hackle feather and a length of Green Peacock Herl. A section of a mallard blue wing feather is also tied in and the tying silk wound back near the eye.
2. The peacok herl is wound to form the body.
3. Next, the badger hackle is wound round to form the legs.
4. The mallard feather is brought over the back and we have the finished nymph.

quite enough. Second half of body is also peacock herl and the head hackle, also Rhode Island Red is wound on long-shanked No. 8 or No. 10 hook.

Second is Baby Doll, which is a lure composed entirely of white wool. Tail is well teased out to make it bushy. Body: two lengths are wound round and the back is also made of two lengths of wool. The brightest of white wool is best. I use "Sirdar".

The last of this new trio is basically a hair-fly. Body is composed of black wool or floss silk ribbed with oval or flat silver tinsel wound to near the hook eye, then a couple of turns of fluorescent magenta wool is tied in. The throat hackle is black squirrel tail and the wing is also composed of this.

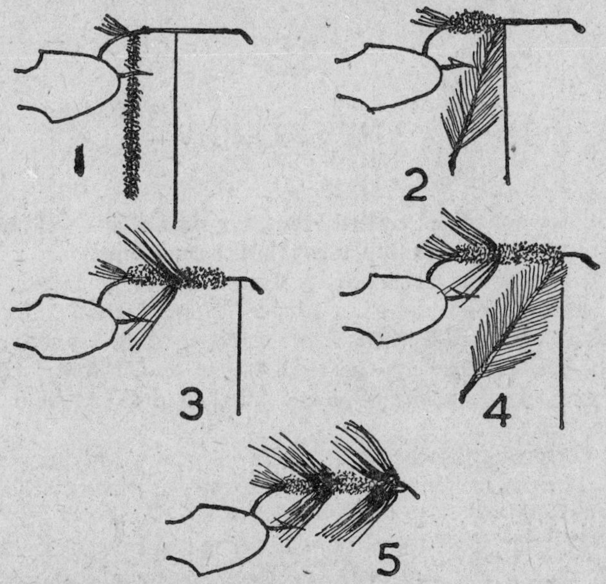

Fig. 28 Dressing the Dambuster

1. A No. 8 or 10 long-shanked hook is in the vice and a tail of bright yellow wool, teased out into strands is tied in together with three strands of peacock herl. The black tying silk is wound to half-way along the shank.
2. A Rhode Island cock hackle is tied in.
3. The hackle is wound and tied off and three more lengths of peacock herl are wound on the shank to near the hook eye.
4. A second Rhode Island Red hackle is tied in.
5. The fly is now complete with a black varnished head.

For several years now I have had a rod on a well-stocked side stream of the River Test, near Romsey, which flows through the estate of Lord Mountbatten, and my largest rainbow to date is an 8½-pounder that fell to the peacock beetle.

In concluding this chapter, it is only right to point out that many brown trout patterns of wet, dry and also nymphs take their quota of rainbows each season, but don't forget to have a few lures and streamers in your box.

19

THE SALMON

It was as a schoolboy that I caught my first salmon – although it would be more truthful to say the fish caught me.

Home for the spring holiday, I was "drowning" a worm in a beautiful pool of the River Llugwy (North Wales), when the salmon struck. The shock to my nervous system was such that my hands "froze" to the rod and reel and, before I could regain any semblance of mental poise, the fish had me in the pool with it.

Fortunately another angler nearby saw my plight, jumped in and helped me out of the pool, the water of which reached to my shoulders.

Through it all I kept hold of the rod and twenty minutes after the salmon had hooked itself my new-found friend gaffed it – twelve pounds.

From that day I have always respected the strength and fighting ability of *Salmo salar*.

However, after all these years, during which time I have made a careful study of the salmon and his near kinsman, the sea-trout, I must confess that my knowledge of the pair is very little. Indeed, on more than one occasion I have thought, in my ignorance, the answer to a particular problem had been reached, when in fact all that had happened was a "gate" had been opened to confront me with other far more difficult questions. And so it will go on to the end of time, for these two species, like so many others, are "unsolved riddles". Of one fact I am sure, which is that the Creator lost the mould after He had fashioned the salmon and sea trout, for no greater aquatic fighters exist in these islands.

Today a lot of people, including many anglers, still think that to indulge in salmon and sea trout fishing requires, first and foremost, a good bank account. Fortunately, that is not so. I grant that a large percentage of the best fishing is held by landowners or leased for fabulous sums to private individuals or syndicates. Despite all this there are still hundreds of miles of good ticket water in these Isles where a visitor, given a little luck with water and weather conditions, can still kill a salmon, or perhaps two or three for a reasonable fee per week. Ten years ago you could obtain salmon fishing for as little as fifty pence per week in Wales and Scotland, but I am afraid those days have gone for ever.

Of course the angler has to know something about tackle and the species he hopes to catch.

For instance, I have been amazed at the number of anglers who have difficulty in identifying a salmon. Others have little or no idea how to go about locating salmon or sea trout lies on strange waters.

A few months before I started to write this book a friend was fishing with me on a Scottish river and landed a 12¾lb, bull trout and honestly thought he had caught a specimen brown trout.

Then again, there are scores of problems and pitfalls to ensnare the novice and the unwary. I do not know all the answers, but I am confident that what I have to say in the chapters which follow will form a sound basis upon which the newcomer can start his fishing career.

Those of us who yearly pit our skills against these silver gamesters have all had strange experiences when fishing. For myself, there have been many occasions when salmon have appeared ravenous, striking at anything that landed in the water, then in an instant the water is dead, with no movement whatsoever.

On one memorable occasion not so many years ago I was fishing the Tweed along with a couple of friends, all within a hundred yards of each other when, at practically the same moment, we each hooked a salmon, and strangely enough each fish was landed without snarling lines. However, the strange thing about this occurrence was that my fish – 18¾ lb – was caught on eel-tail, a 23 pounder succumbed to a spoon, and a 14 lb fish fell for the lure of a sea trout size Durham Ranger. Salmon are like that; you never can tell what they will fancy to strike at. The man who has faith in a particular fly or bait will always take a fish or two during a season, but the most successful angler will be he who is observant and is able to match his fishing with the conditions prevailing.

On every water there will be periods ideal for the fly and the same can be said for natural baits, spoons and spinners, not forgetting that most humble of salmon and sea trout baits, the worm.

20

NATURAL HISTORY OF SALMON AND A FEW PERILS

Of all the many chapters that go to make up the great book of Nature, none is of greater interest than that of the salmon. Nature still holds inviolate much of the salmon's history, particularly that dealing with its life in the sea. However, we do know from angling experience that each and every member of the salmon tribe is an amalgam of odd contrasts.

From birth till death the salmon struggles against circumstances; a fight which countless thousands lose. In the sea they are preyed upon by innumerable foes, and on entering the tidal stretches of our river system they have to face their most deadly enemy – man.

Before they can reach home, the headwaters of the river in which they were born, they must first run the gauntlet of nets of varying designs, all calculated to stop as many of the silver warriors as possible.

Those that get through then face other perils. Anglers with the finest tackle that science and engineering skill can produce take their toll of the travellers, along with the poachers with their nets, snares, barbed gaffs, explosives and poisons.

Eventually a pitiful few reach their destination, the spawning grounds used by the forebears, there to procreate the species. Even then there is no let up in their slaughter, for poachers raid the spawning beds at night.

Egg-laden females are the most valuable to these thieves and are killed by the score. Stripped of their eggs, their flesh finds a ready sale in the black market, while the eggs are salted down and usually sold in one pound jars to individuals who have the audacity to call themselves anglers.

To me, the taking of a spawning fish is the greatest crime

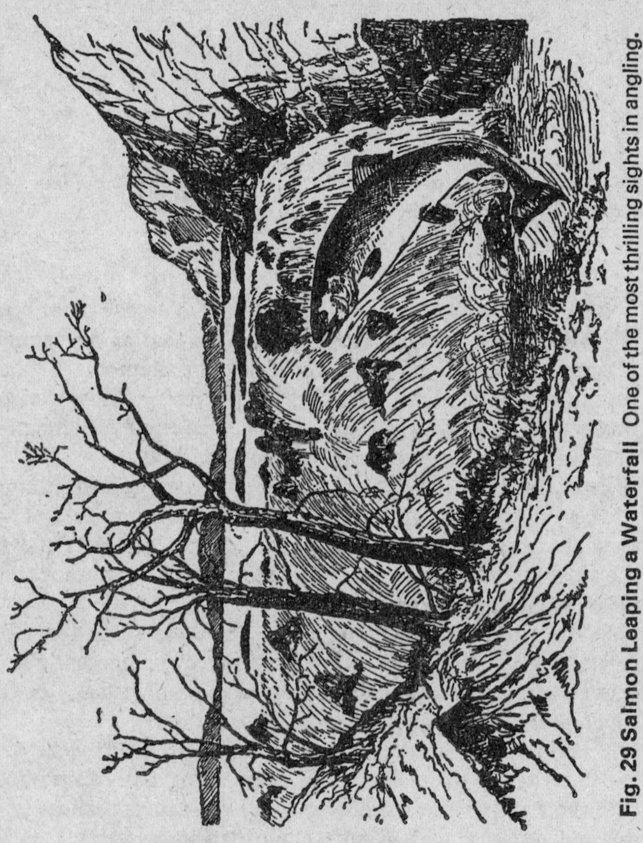

Fig. 29 Salmon Leaping a Waterfall One of the most thrilling sights in angling.

of all, and should be treated as such by those who administer the laws. Far too often river keepers and watchers are not above suspicion in this respect.

But to return: their task of spawning completed, many salmon die from exhaustion, parasites and disease. The remainder, emaciated and weak, face the dangers of the return journey. Again, the chief of those perils is the poacher and secondly, the angler who has not taken the trouble to distinguish between a clean fish and a kelt (unclean fish). Thousands

Fig. 30 A Salmon

of kelts are killed every season by anglers who should have known better. Many clubs and associations have a clause in their rules prohibiting the use of a gaff, both at the commencement of a season and also nearing the close.

Until a few years ago no man could say with certainty where the Atlantic Salmon fed in the sea. Today we know that most of our salmon have their feeding grounds off Greenland. For centuries Nature kept her secret, but commercial fishermen, with the aid of electronics, wrested it from her. Since it was discovered, many thousands of tons of salmon have been caught in nets by the Danes. The slaughter eventually became so bad that this country, along with many others, protested, but I am sorry to say the netting continues. A direct result has been that many of our rivers have had reduced runs.

I am sorry to say that man, as a whole, is greedy, and rarely thinks of the future. To scoop such numbers from the sea as well as tidal waters has done irreparable harm to angling and will continue to do so. Man is ruthless, particularly where the end product is money.

Now let us look a little closer at salmon when spawning, Contrary to what many think, the cock (male) fish does little or no work in making ready the redd. The hen (female) does the hard graft with nose and tail.

When a suitable spot is found, the hen scoops out a channel with nose and tail, lays in the channel and releases a pocket of eggs, moves away and the male fish moves in and fertilises them. The hen then covers them up with sand and gravel and makes another channel in which to release another pocket of eggs and so on, until the two skeins of eggs she has been carrying have been shed. The spawning process may take anything from a week to a month, and usually takes place at night and is accompanied with loud splashing as the hen fans her tail, making and covering up the redds.

Salmon about to spawn have a particular colouration: the male fish loses his silvery coat, which is replaced by a reddish colour with red stripes and splotches on gill covers and back. The bottom jaw develops a hook at the nose and altogether he is an ugly-looking fellow. His flesh that was so red in the spring, is now a pale pink and is tasteless. As the milt (fertilising fluid) ripens, so does the flesh deteriorate until at the time of actual spawning the fish is deemed unclean.

The hen also changes in colour. The silver and purples on back and flanks give way to a dark grey colouration, until by the time she starts shedding her eggs she is nearly black on the back with dark grey flanks.

The salmon is not a prolific breeder. A ten-pounder would produce about 6,000 to 7,000 eggs. Of these only a small percentage ever reach the sea as salmon, hence the need for conserving what we have.

In fresh water it has four stages, the egg, fry, parr, and smolt. It is fairly easy to tell a smolt due to its silvery coat, but the parr is not so easy due to its trout-like appearance.

A salmon parr has ten to twelve parr marks crossing the lateral line with ten to twelve rays in dorsal fin. The fins are usually of a greyish tinge, and there are two or three dark spots on the gill covers. The tail is deeply cleft.

A young trout has nine or ten parr marks, the dorsal fin has eight to ten rays. The adipose fin is red and the others are an orange colour with a reddish tinge. There are numerous spots on the gill covers and the tail is only slightly cleft.

Salmon parr are particularly active during spring and summer and at times are a nuisance when dry-fly fishing for trout, so take the utmost care when releasing them. Who knows, you may be lucky and hook the same fish in one, two or three years' time when it returns to the river as a grilse (maiden salmon), in which case it will then be a fish of anything from five to seven pounds. When a fish enters a river to spawn a second time it is called a salmon. The colouration of a grilse is silver overlaid with a purplish sheen, the tail is slightly cleft. The salmon proper is coloured bright silver and has a square tail.

Anglers and others interested often ponder about the salmon's ability to locate the river of its birth. At one time not so very long ago it was thought the homing of the salmon was by instinct, but today it is known that its nose plays a great part in this strangest of all characteristics of this species. Nature has equipped the salmon's organ of smell with as fine a piece of mechanism as any she has created. Inside each

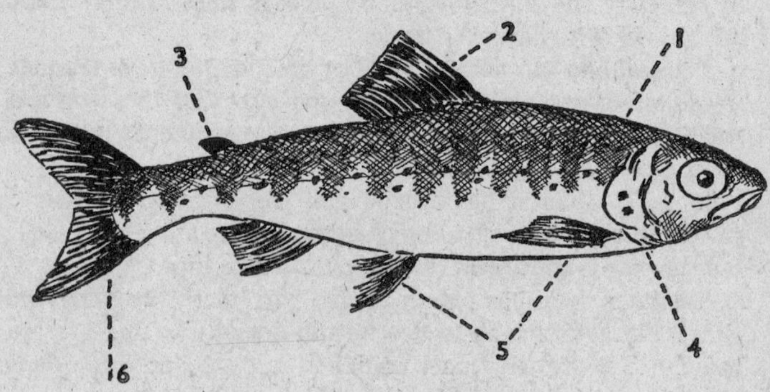

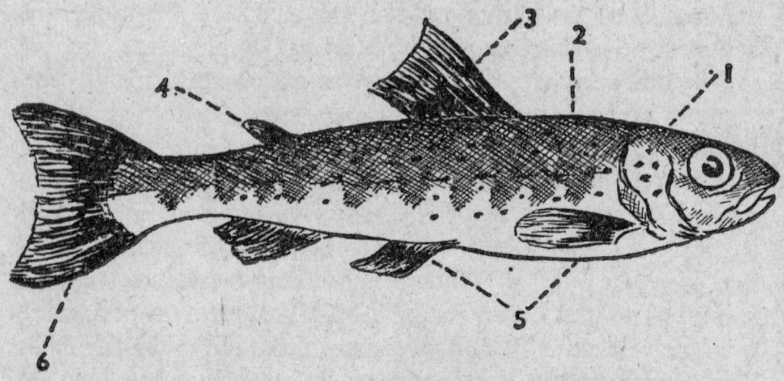

Fig 31 How to Distinguish between Salmon Parr and Young Trout

Salmon (Above)

1. Ten to twelve parr marks
2. Ten to twelve rays
3. Greyish tinge
4. Two or three spots on gill cover
5. Grey colour
6. Deeply cleft tail

Trout (Below)

1. Numerous spots on gill cover
2. Nine or ten parr marks
3. Eight to ten rays
4. Orange colour
5. Orange colour with reddish tinge
6. Slightly cleft tail

nostril are a number of membraneous folds with nerve fronds emanating from each one. The nerves receive the smell impressions and pass them on to the folds which act as amplifiers. Once the salmon picks up the smell of its home river he follows it up. Thus homing instinct, coupled with power of smell, enable it to make the journey home.

To assist the salmon to reach the spawning beds Nature, in many instances, has provided ladders in the shape of falls, but where these are missing man has put in artificial ladders.

Fig. 32 A Natural Fish Ladder River Balgy (Scotland) near Loch Torridon

Waterfalls and ladders are the places to observe salmon on the run. The sight is one never to forget, and particularly to a townsman it brings surprise and wonder.

As I mentioned earlier in this chapter, the salmon is an amalgam of odd contrasts. Many writers, yes even scientists, have stated that they do not feed in fresh-water. That some salmon do feed when in a river I have proved over and over again. I have caught salmon in England, Wales, Scotland, and Ireland with quantities of partly digested worms inside them, while on other occasions they have had minnows and night flies in the stomach. I am not saying it is a general rule, for Nature has dictated it otherwise. It stands to reason that if salmon always fed in rivers there would not be any food left for the other residents. Instead of saying "they do not feed in fresh-water" it would be far better to compromise, for Nature has a habit of making liars of us all at some time or other in our individual careers.

In the sea the food of a salmon is composed mainly of prawns, shrimps, sand-eels and the young of other fish. Thus we get an idea of the baits to use.

21

IDENTIFYING THE CATCH

To those who have caught many salmon the title of this chapter may seem silly, but believe me it is far from that. In my travels I have come across many anglers who have been puzzled by the fish they have caught. For instance, a few years ago I was fishing the Coquet when an angler came along and displayed a lovely fish which he honestly believed was a salmon; actually it was a 12½ lb sea trout. Time and again since then that has happened.

Then again, I have heard the bull trout referred to as a salmon trout and also a sea trout.

There are, of course, several ways of making sure that the fish caught is a salmon. The tail is a good guide to start with. That of a grilse is slightly cleft, but that of a salmon proper is square. Then we have the spots, which in a salmon and also a grilse, are always above the lateral line, but in a sea trout there are more spots with many below the lateral line, while the bull trout is practically covered with spots.

The gill covers of salmon (which of course, includes grilse) are different from those of sea trout and bull trout.

The tail of a sea trout invariably has a cleft in it, but on reaching eight to ten pounds it is not so pronounced.

The bull trout has a round tail, and in many parts of the North-East it is often referred to as the round tail. Very often I have seen bull trout offered for sale as sea trout. The fishmonger, maybe, did not know the difference and twice in recent years I have seen them on sale as salmon, the tail having been carefully shaped with a pair of scissors. The flesh of the bull trout is tasteless and is yellowish in colour.

Several scientific writers on British fish life have referred to the bull trout as just another local name for sea trout. Granted, it is of the trout family and goes to sea, but there the

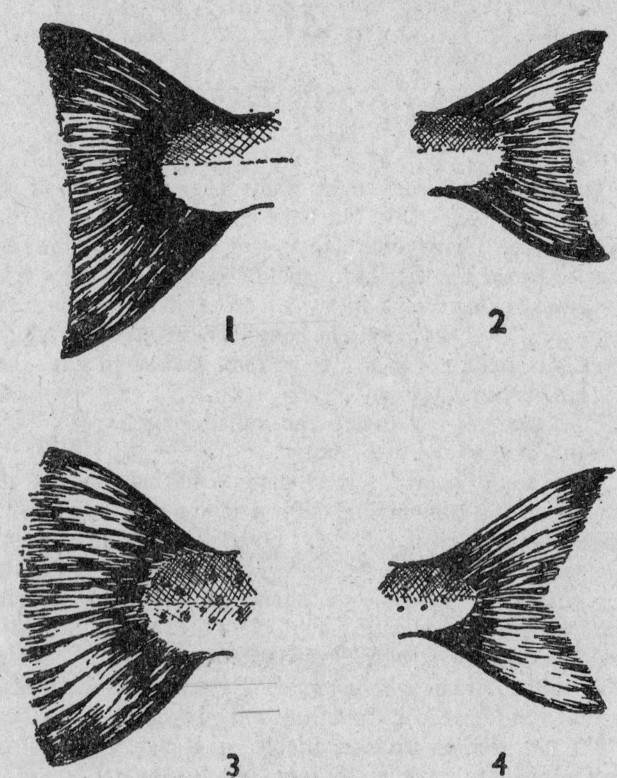

Fig. 33 What a Tail Can Tell
1. Tail of a Salmon
2. The slightly forked tail of a Grilse
3. Round tail of a Bull Trout
4. Sea Trout Tail

likeness ends, for the bull trout is nothing like a sea trout, even when you get them of two and three pounds. It is my belief, based on years of study at the riverside, that this ocean-loving trout is a breed that has evolved over countless centuries from the ordinary brown trout. You have only to see a sea trout and a bull trout side by side to note the difference, for it is most obvious.

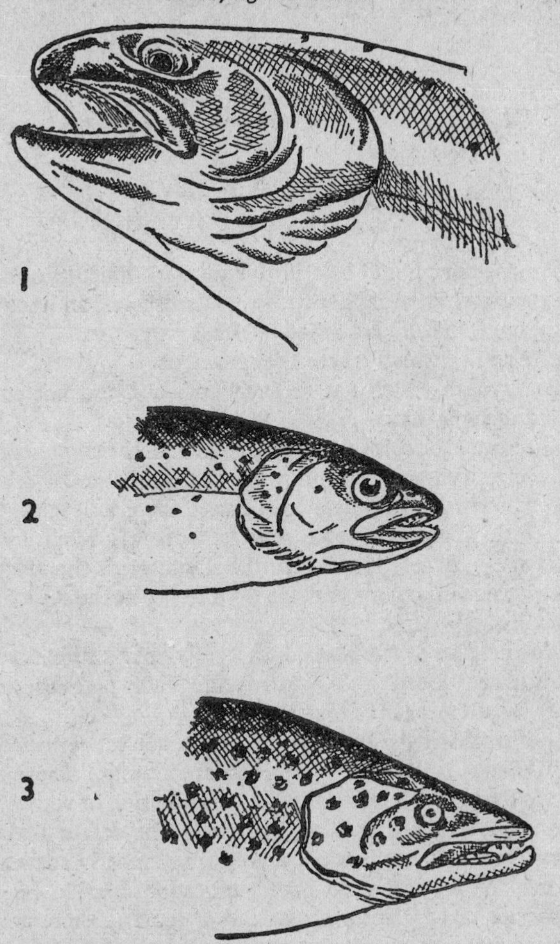

Fig 34 Gill Cover Identification
1. Salmon 2. Sea Trout 3. Bull Trout

Its name, bull trout, gives some indication of its disposition towards most of the other residents of pool and stream. Only one thing can be said in its favour, and that is, it fights well when hooked.

22

IS IT A KELT?

In the spring and also in the autumn difficulties may arise in the differentiating between a clean fish and an unclean one. An "unclean fish" is defined by the Act to mean:

1. Any fish which is about to spawn, or
2. Any fish which has recently spawned and not recovered from spawning.

The onus for correct decision rests with the angler concerned in every case, and the following characteristics by which unclean fish may generally be recognised are as follows:

1. Fish about to spawn (end of season). Their outline is unshapely, developing depth of belly towards the vent. Males turn a reddish colour and the bottom jaw at the nose develops a hook or gib.

In the case of the female, the belly shows fullness and the vent, in advanced cases, protrusion. Slight pressure on flanks may cause emission of ova (eggs).

2. Fish that have spawned and have not yet returned to the sea (kelts). In shape they are emaciated, weight disproportionate to length with distension or inflammation of vent. The fins are usually ragged as is also the tail. The colour is dark and dirty, but on occasions, especially with an early spawned fish, it may be silvery when other indications should be sought. The gills are a dirty pink instead of red and there are nearly always maggots present at the tips, whereas those of a clean fish are nearly always free from maggots.

In contrast to a fish from the sea, a kelt's mouth is full of sharp teeth.

Bearing these facts in mind, it is always best to tail your fish out at the early and latter part of a season. A sympathetic bailiff may come along, but again the official may not be so kindly disposed. Loss of the licence and one's good name as

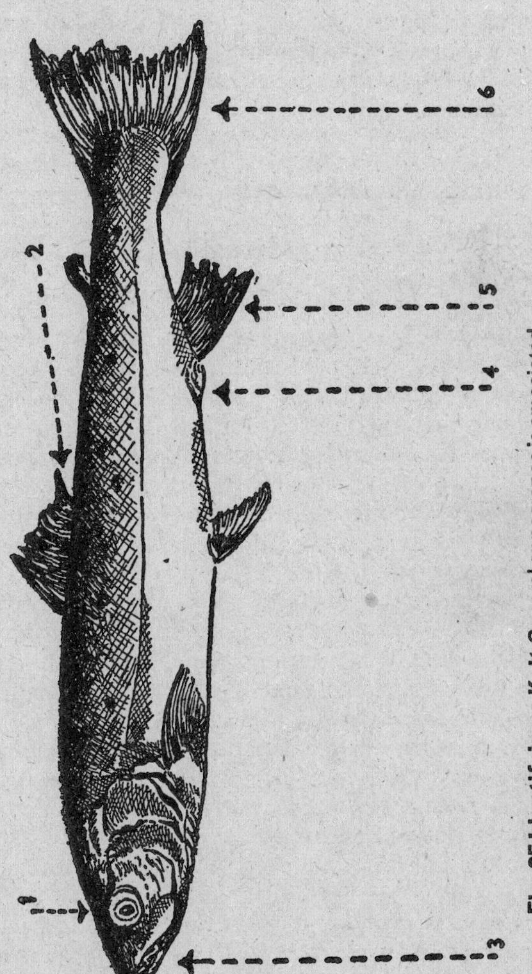

Fig. 35 Identifying a Kelt General appearance is emaciated

1. Large and protruding eye
2. Ragged dorsal fin
3. Large teeth at front of mouth
4. Inflamed vent
5. Torn anal fin
6. Badly torn on frayed tail

an angler usually follows. Surely it is not worth the risk when a little study and thought was all that was necessary to prevent it. Once the gaff goes home it is much too late to start worrying whether it is a kelt or not. Far better to lose a clean fish in the tailing out process than use a gaff when you do not know whether it is a clean fish or not. If you are in doubt, release the fish at once and offer up a silent prayer for better luck next time.

23

LOCATING THE BEST LIES

Unless floods alter the bed of a river, successive generations of salmon will occupy the same lies when resting in pools en route for the spawning grounds. Occasionally, when winter in all its storm-swept fury floods a river, things are altered. Boulders and rocks are dislodged and deposited elsewhere and the whole character of the river bed is changed.

Salmon like plenty of cover, particularly during the hours of daylight, and if a pool is devoid of the right protection they will travel, providing the water is suitable, onward to the next pool. If conditions are not right for them to continue up stream, they will fall back to a lower pool. It stands to reason, therefore, that the angler who can, at a glance, read the potentialities of a pool is much better equipped for taking a fish than the angler who has to use the most tiresome of methods – trial and error.

No matter what water you are on, river or loch, there are "signposts" providing you are observant enough to see them. It is far better to spend an hour studying the water one is going to fish than putting the tackle up and wasting energy in practically useless casting.

On private stretches the ghillie or keeper acts as the interpreter of these signs and directs the angler's attentions to what he considers to be the most productive places. The "ticket" angler on a strange water has to discover them himself, and it can be a long and tiresome job, because locals are not keen on divulging the best lies.

Early season salmon, that is, as far as my experience goes, prefer holes of from five to eight feet deep, with plenty of rocks to shelter them from strong under currents. A bend in a river's course where the stream has cut a deep hole is always a likely spot for resting salmon. It is practically useless to look for spring salmon in anything but quiet pools during the

Fig. 36 Where Salmon lie in Rivers
1. Deep shady pools 2. Near sunken rocks 3. Deep pool 4. Rocky Stream

daytime. In the twilight they move up into the streams, for the purpose of cleaning themselves in the sand and gravel. As soon as it is daylight back to the pools they go.

Periodically during the daytime they go for an exercise swim up and down the stream, circling their lie. It is usually when a salmon is so engaged that he takes the angler's offering. In pools near estuaries where the pull of the tide is felt, I have found that the salmon respond by cruising around the pool, so it is always a good idea to have a tide table with you.

The surface of a pool will give an indication of the bed. A boil is usually the sign of a submerged rock at a good depth. Where a huge boulder rears its hoary head above the water, which in turn roars past on either side of it, there will, nine times out of ten, be good depth and a gravel bottom. The largest fish in the pool invariably takes up residence at such a place.

Deep channels, overhung by trees and bushes, in which there are plenty of rocks and shaded pools, are all good spots that the angler should explore.

When a river is rising it is always a good time to try for a fish and also as it is approaching its normal level. Salmon rarely strike when on the run. I have caught salmon when running, but they have been foul-hooked. Whether they turned at the fly, missed, and were hooked as it went past, I do not know.

A few years ago while fishing the River Balgy, Scotland, I foul-hooked two salmon and a sea trout one after the other and the bailiff, Mr. J. Sutherland, told me that he had seen it happen many times during a flood, but he had yet to see a fish take the fly in its mouth.

A good fly water after a flood is when it is the colour of light ale. This stage is reached two or three days before the water becomes normal. The mud, sand and other suspended matter has settled and the fish are very often moving around full of vigour, due to the extra oxygen in the water. When a water becomes low the oxygen content falls and the only movement out of the fish will be their exercise cruises during the daytime, but they will be in the deep streamy water in the evening.

In lochs, the deep overshadowed sections are always worth a cast or two and particular attention should be paid to the streamy

Fig. 37 Salmon lies in a Loch

1. Deep overshadowed water 2. Off rocky headlands 3. Near feeder streams

and fast water one usually finds sweeping past rocky headlands. Where there are feeder streams there are invariably sand and gravel bars lying at good depth: these are worth always a cast or two. Loch fishing is nearly always boat work, so it is fairly safe to assume that you will have a local with you who should know the best spots, but even so always bear in mind the kind of holding places mentioned. The boatman may be honest enough, but then again he may be taking out a client the following day who tips fairly heavily if he catches a salmon. Such things have happened and will happen again for it is the frailty of human nature, therefore it is always best to have a shot or two in your own locker in case the boatman fails to produce the goods.

24

TACKLE PROBLEMS

Many anglers just starting to fish for salmon overlook an important factor. It is that for the proper functioning of rod, reel and line, the three units should be as one when in use. In other words, they should be balanced so that the angler is not unduly tired or the tackle strained.

A split cane rod with too heavy a line will soon develop a "set" while a rod with too light a line will never cast well or to any great distance. A reel with too much weight strains both wrist and forearm. Bearing these simple things in mind, it is best to seek the advice of someone who has experience in these matters. Usually rod makers advocate certain reels and lines for a particular type of rod and the novice should take heed.

Sixty years ago we had sixteen and eighteen foot rods and reels of brass and bronze together with heavy lines to balance them. Wielding such tools can be very tiresome and as fishing became more and more popular the rod makers started to experiment with lighter rods and reels. Today we have salmon fly rods of built cane, fibre glass and graphite of twelve and thirteen feet, but rarely above fourteen feet. Such rods are capable of whipping the largest fish, providing of course, the angler behind the rod knows his job.

For fly fishing the line should be double tapered, not less than thirty yards in length and this should be spliced to braided nylon of not less than eighteen pounds. The total capacity of the reel should never be less than one hundred yards. Indeed, on occasions you may wish you had more line to play with – I have more than once.

In my early days after salmon we used silk-worm gut leaders and to get the taper one had to use knots, which of course weakened it. Also, they had to be damped before use.

Today one can purchase leaders that are tapered in one length without the unsightly knots. Another point in favour of nylon is that it does not fray as easily as natural gut or perish due to an overdose of sunlight or damp.

Flies must be kept in proper containers to protect the points, barbs and feathers. Such boxes equipped with clips are fairly cheap and last a lifetime.

You can please yourself regarding a gaff. Some anglers I know never use one, preferring to tail their fish out by hand. As a matter of fact my wife has not used a gaff for years. She plays the fish right out, then with a handkerchief-covered hand, grasps the fish at the wrist (the slim portion next to the tail) and drags it to the bankside. For my part I feel half-naked if my gaff (a telescopic one) is not hanging at my side. However, at the start and near the end of a season I use a tailer.

A container for spoons and spinning baits is also advisable, but for goodness sake do not start collecting such items. Remember the beauty of fishing can only be enjoyed to its fullest extent if one is travelling light. If you start collecting all manner of flies and artificial baits the time will most certainly come when your fishing will become so complicated that you will waste valuable fishing time trying this and that. The manufacturers flood the shops with all manner of weird and wonderful things, all calculated to catch salmon, but that does not mean to say you have to purchase them. There are old and tried flies, spoons and spinners and if the angler sticks to them he will not go far wrong.

You will want waders or thigh boots. Here again, it is a matter for the individual.

When the water is not in good fly order the spinning rod comes into its own. My rod is 8½ feet built cane, but my wife and son use fibre glass and swear by it. Our reels, however, are the same – Altex, but there are dozens of fixed spool reels on the market, some good and some not so good. Whatever tackle you purchase get that which has a name and tradition behind it, for a penny wise can very often be a pound foolish.

In the last five years braided nylon and nylon monofil has superseded silk lines. I prefer twelve pound braided nylon for salmon and four pound monofil for sea trout, which means you will need a spare drum for your reel. The modern reel is so made that a drum can be changed in a couple of minutes. At the moment monofil over ten pounds is often difficult to handle due to it being springy, and when the bail-arm is lifted preparatory to making a cast, if one is not careful it flies off the drum in coils and valuable time is wasted in unravelling and winding it back on. Sometimes it gets into such a tangle that a length has to be cut off.

Multiplying reels (an American invention) can handle any kind of monofil, but fail on the question of spare drums and the ease with which they are changed.

Of course, if you have plenty of money to burn you can have a reel for salmon and another for sea trout, but look at the bulk you are building up, not forgetting the extra weight. For my part the fixed spool reel has my vote every time for a good one is practically foolproof.

The man who made spinning (thread-lining if you like) so popular for taking salmon and sea trout was Alexander Wanless. He had to face considerable opposition in his fight to get spinning recognised as a sporting method, but before he died he had the satisfaction of seeing its popularity grow by leaps and bounds until today practically every salmon angler is equipped with thread-line tackle as it was called in those days.

I met him twice in Scotland while fishing and derived much benefit from our short acquaintance. Would that we could have met years earlier then quite a few of my problems with spinning rod and reel would have been answered.

25

FLY FISHING

Sometimes the beginner at salmon fishing is awed by the talk of experts and receives the impression that in perhaps fifty years, if he reads all the books and studies hard, he might learn to cast a fly and even catch a salmon. Nonsense. One of the most disheartening things to the novice is the mass of misinformation, distorted facts and unproved theories concerning his tackle and fishing methods. Why such a grand sport should be surrounded by so much baloney is hard to understand.

To clear away some of the clouds, it is my contention that the two characteristics that go to make up a good angler with the salmon fly are perception and adaptability.

The man who can cast a trout fly can, with a little practice, cast a creditable line for salmon, It does not necessarily follow that one has to cast a long line to lure a fish. Very often the fish are lying close in and casts have to be made when standing back from the water's edge. Some anglers appear to think that wading is essential to get to the best lies. A very dear friend of mine who taught me quite a lot about fly fishing has never had a pair of waders in his life. In the forty years I knew him he always wore Wellingtons and his record of salmon on the fly runs into several hundred. Mind you, his best periods were before the rivers were so commercialised or polluted. However, a pair of waders or thigh boots are handy in case of trouble such as snagging, etc.

Never overload yourself with too many fly patterns or else the time will most surely come when you will spend more time changing flies than you do fishing. I know because I went through the "grasshopper" minded stage early on in my career. Fortunately the habit was arrested before it became too deep-seated. Today my box contains twenty-four flies, but there are

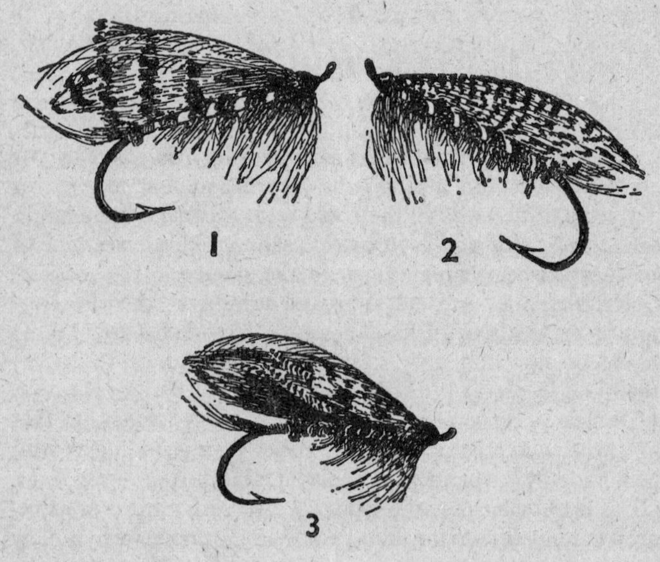

Fig. 38 Some Famous Salmon Flies

1. Durham Ranger
2. Fiery Brown
3. Jock Scott
4. Wilkinson
5. Grey Turkey

only twelve individual patterns because they are dressed in two sizes. Large, for early fishing and use in tidal pools, and smaller ones for general river fishing. On occasion I have had recourse to sea trout flies like many other salmon anglers.

Salmon fly patterns I can vouch for are Durham Ranger, Fiery Brown, Jock Scott, Wilkinson, Grey Turkey, Blue Charm, Thunder and Lightning, Curry's Shrimp, Common Shrimp, Woolly Shrimp, Spring Grub and Jungle Grub. The two sizes are: For tidal and heavy water No. 2, which is about $1\frac{1}{8}$ inch long and for ordinary river work No. 6, the length which is about $\frac{13}{16}$ inch. All the hooks I use are "ordinary forged" and are black enamelled with up-turned eyes. This type of hook (iron some people call it) has served me well and I have no hesitation in recommending it. The sheath of enamel prevents rust, which is a good thing particularly when fishing brackish water.

If a nylon leader is being used, my advice is use the knot illustrated in the sketch. Actually, it is a combination of two knots, for a simple knot is tied, then after the required loops have been done, the whole is pulled tight and the simple knot, which is a safety device of my own, prevents any slipping of the main knot. I use this type of knot for all types of fishing when using nylon as a cast or trace and it has never let me down yet. Some idea of its strength can be gauged from the fact that it stood up to the tremendous pressure exerted by fifty pound tarpon when I was fly fishing for them in Florida some years ago, and believe me, a silver king (tarpon) has forgotten more tricks than a salmon will ever know.

In Scotland I have come across quite a number of anglers who use two flies to a leader, but that, to my way of thinking is asking for a load of trouble if you hook a fish of any weight at all. The flashing runs and dives of a hooked salmon are bad enough to control without having to worry as to whether the second fly is going to snag. A few months before this book was planned, I was fishing a Scottish Highland river, and rounding a bend, I found an angler fast to a good fish, which every now and then took to the air. There was a large bed of weed on the opposite side of the pool and in a tremendous burst of energy the fish found sanctuary there. The angler was using a leader

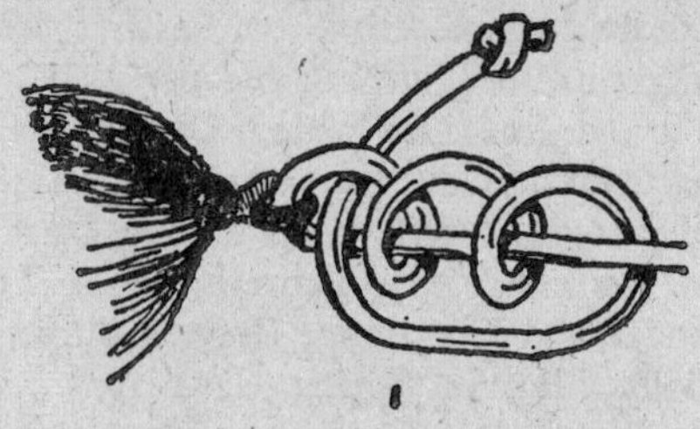

1

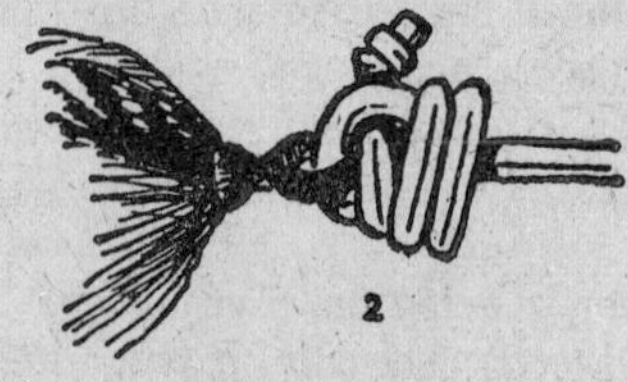

2

Fig. 39 A Safe Knot for Nylon Leaders and Traces
1. Two-turn Blood with simple knot at end
2. When pulled tight it has 85% strength and never slips

of two flies, and the one that was trailing got tangled up. The last we saw of that fish was a leap, in which all his weight fell on the tight leader, resulting in the salmon regaining its well-earned freedom. It took the annoyed angler about ten minutes to get his line and leader back minus a fly.

In fig. 41 are illustrations of some flies that are not so widely used as they should be. They are ideal for both spring use and in the autumn. Curry's Shrimp is one of the best patterns I know for use in tidal pools, just as the tide is approaching the flood stage. Large sea trout are also lured by it in brackish water.

The Common and Woolly Shrimps are at times deadly; early morning, in the streamy water during periods of drought or fished at night for sea trout, they have been known to hold their own with more famous patterns.

My son, when fishing in Ireland last season, had reasonable success when using Waddington Thunder, Jungle-Alexandra,

Fig. 40 Occasional Flies
1. Waddington Thunder
2. Jungle-Alexandra
3. Junglecock and Silver

and Junglecock and Silver. I have never done much with them and for that reason they are not included in my box, but he uses them fairly often and for that reason they are included here. As I have said many times before, faith has a lot to do with one's success with fly or bait.

Maybe I am prejudiced against the Waddington type of dressing because I once saw a man deliberately foul-hook a salmon with this kind of fly. The fish was lying, and had been for some days, beside a rock near to the bank and was easy to see. This individual, for I cannot call him an angler, dropped his fly in the water, brought it alongside the fish and struck, foul-hooking the fish in the flank. I am pleased to record that the fish regained its freedom and the man involved had his licence withdrawn.

Occasionally one may foul-hook a fish when fly fishing, but that is vastly different to driving in the hook deliberately and I am afraid that treble-hooked flies have put into the hands of the unscrupulous a means of taking fish other than by fair angling. Unless the deed is actually witnessed no one can say whether it was deliberate or not. That is the tragedy of it, for these types of lures are legitimate.

In salmon fly fishing more so than any other kind the angler must persevere. Far too often fishermen give a cast or two on a pool then move off to another spot. Never be in too much hurry to see what is round the next bend. In all probability the pool that has been casually fished holds the most prospects, but the fly was not getting down or was not just what the fish were looking for. I could quote dozens of instances where a pool has been partially fished and then along would come an angler who stuck to his job and was rewarded with a salmon.

Another point is that some people fail to realise the importance of angles and fish each pool in the same way. They have a stereotyped pattern and forget a simple fact that from some angles fish can see you and from others they are blind to the presence of anyone nearby. After a pool has been fished from one angle it should be rested for an hour at least and then the fly should be put across from an entirely different angle.

It is also a good thing to remember that the easy to reach places will have been flogged to death, therefore the man who

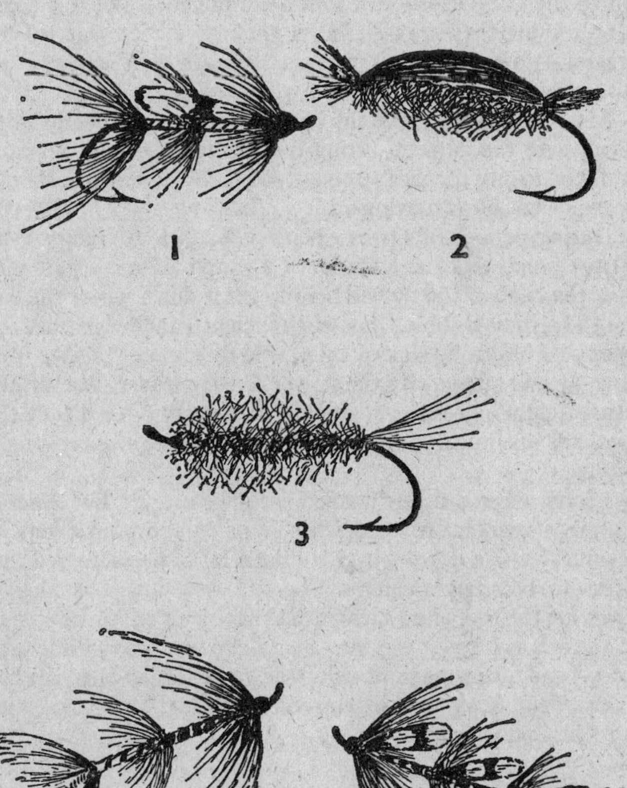

Fig. 41 Shrimps and Grubs

1. Curry's Shrimp
2. Common Shrimp
3. Woolly Shrimp
4. Spring Grub
5. Jungle Grub

exploits the more difficult spots has the better chance of a rise. Occasionally it may mean lying on your belly to reach a lie, but you will invariably find that the trouble entailed is well worth the extra exertion. Salmon are not fools (even if some people think they are), and after they have been worried for several days they select a spot that is more quiet and appears secure.

Always cast well above the likely places and let the fly work down with the current, lifting the rod top a few inches now and then to give the fly a semblance of "life". Every inch should be explored before moving on.

During periods of spates when the water is running strong I have found that the addition of a couple of small split shot near the head of the fly will help to get it down where the fish are. The only trouble when such weight is added is that the back cast has to be slowed up a little to counter-balance it or your fly will tangle with the slower moving leader. I never like using weight on a cast but circumstances very often dictate the methods one must use if the bag is to feel the pleasant weight of a fish.

Lastly, when a fish is hooked keep the rod up, but lower it to near horizontal when the fish leaps. A rod that is kept at about forty-five degrees exerts quite a lot of pressure and that pressure becomes greater as the fish weakens. The idea of lowering the rod when a leap takes place is to offset the weight of the fish as it re-enters the water. Keep cool (most difficult, I know) and take your time, using the gaff or tailer when the fish shows definite signs of exhaustion by rolling on its side with bubbles issuing from its mouth.

26

USING THE FLOATING LINE

Invented in the first place for a particular type of water and then adapted by a number of anglers for use all through the season, floating line fishing is not so widely practised as it should be. It has saved the day for me on quite a number of occasions when the more orthodox methods, had failed to stir a "fin".

The inventor was the late Mr. A. H. E. Wood of Cairnton and Cashels (Scotland) and his theory was to float the line to the salmon with the fly moving a little distance below the surface. He experimented for years and periodically mention would be made in the Press of some large catch he had made. As a result tackle manufacturers started putting out "low water" flies dressed on fine wired hooks and longish shanks. The dressing on such flies is roughly about half of a normal fly.

While Wood's method can be used throughout the whole season, its greatest asset is that it is most successful during periods of brilliant sunshine and fairly low water, and in this respect it should also have a great appeal for dry fly trout anglers.

Every angler knows the problem of trying to take a fish during periods of brilliant sunshine in late June, July, August and September. The streams are thin and fairly smooth of surface, affording the fish clear visibility while the pools are still and the surface like a mirror.

Greased line angling, as it was then called, is for the most part a "dead fly" process, in that the angler does not impart movement – "life" – to the fly. Briefly, it consists of casting up and across water with a floating line and sinking terminal tackle and fly. The fly drifts quietly downstream and over the most likely spots.

Compared with ordinary fly fishing it is a slow process. As

the fly swings round, slack line is taken in to offset pull which would speed up the movement of the fly, which would be fatal. The more line cast the more water can be covered before pull sets up.

Of course, today we do not have to grease our line. Some years ago the Americans developed a line composed of hair-like nylon threads and covered with plastic, thus was the floating line born and so revolutionised the old style "greased line".

In view of the fact that the line is the object of the angler's attention, it is more practical to use a light-coloured one. To be sure, a dark line will work just as well, but under most light conditions a white line will be more easily seen.

An interesting feature of the method is the manner in which the salmon take the fly. Some, of course, make the usual characteristic rush, followed by a surface boil, but the majority of the strikes are, in reality, not strikes at all – just nibbles. Many of these could easily pass undetected unless the angler is watchful for the slightest indication of activity. Often I have had the end of the line disappear slowly, as though sinking under its own weight. Several fish were lost as a result of my failing to realise what was happening. Now as soon as my line starts to sink and slowly move away I tighten immediately and frequently hook the fish.

With the floating line it is only on very rare occasions that the fly snags on the bottom. If the fly is working near the bottom and touches a rock it usually bobs over it, due no doubt to the surface-riding line holding, as it were, suspended in the water.

For this method, while the rod and reel can be the same as that used for ordinary fly fishing, the cast is very different. In a nutshell it is slack-line work and the angler has to cast so that the line falls onto the surface of the water in a zig-zag pattern, thus enabling the fly to sink and travel a considerable distance before being affected by pull.

Many exponents of the floating line "mend" their line just before pull puts in an appearance. This is done by lifting the rod top and switching the line upstream again which enables the fly to remain in the water much longer than if it was lifted out and another cast made. The "mend" or "switchover" as some anglers call it is not easy to master and requires a lot of practice, but it is well worth the time expended. It took me about a whole season before I could "throw" the necessary loop of line upstream. For rocky, turbulent stretches of water it is an ideal method of exploring with the fly in all the best places.

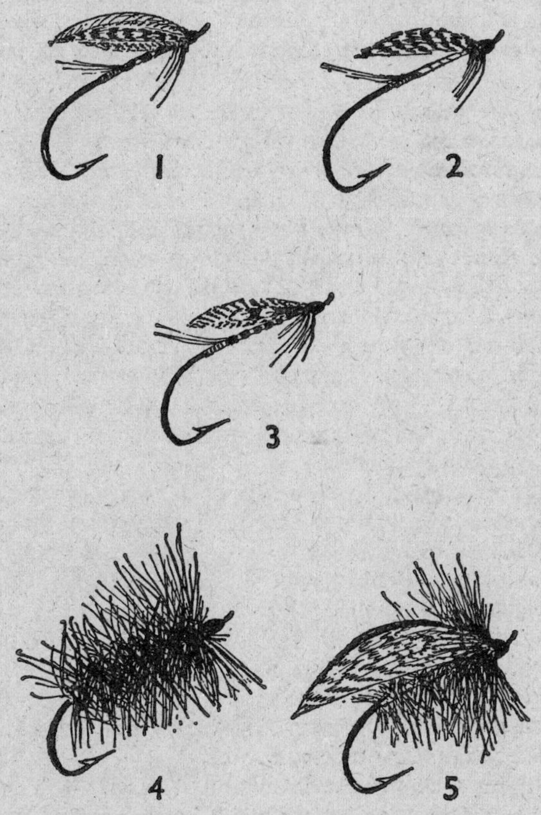

Fig. 42 Low Water and Dry-Flies

1. Blue Charm
2. Blue and Silver
3. Jeannie
4. Black Palmer
5. Cinnamon Sedge

As to fly patterns, my favourites are Blue Charm and Blue and Silver with Jeannie as a standby.

Occasionally when using the floating line you will, in all probability, notice a salmon cruising just beneath the surface, his presence being indicated by an occasional little boil here and there. When such a fish is noticed, change over to the dry-fly and it is quite possible you will connect with him. The dry-flies I like are Black Palmer and Cinnamon Sedge. The former is a good fly to try during the late evening when fish are moving up into the streams for oxygen and an exercise swim.

27

BAIT FISHING

The three natural baits that have accounted for more salmon than any other three are: (1) eel-tail; (2) sprat, gold or silver, and (3) prawn. The first two are early season baits to be used from opening day until the end of April, while the prawn is a summer and autumn bait.

In the early days of a season natural and artificial baits will, by and large, produce more strikes than flies, at least that has been my experience and also that of many of my friends. There is nothing to equal fly-fishing, but there are times when a fly rod can be wielded hour after hour without result. When that happens he is a wise man who changes over to the short rod and spinning tackle.

For the first month or six weeks of a season the first bait I use on every outing is eel-tail. It is tough and even after it has caught a fish or two is still in good condition. One can purchase a jar of preserved sand eels very cheaply, but for my part I much prefer to catch my own and do the preserving myself, and only preserve the four inches, from the tail up to the shoulders, the rest being cut off and thrown away. A pound jam jar will hold a couple of dozen quite easily. For tidal pools I use four inch baits and for general river fishing three inches has proved the best size.

The spinner used by me for years with this bait is the Geen Corkscrew, which has the weight in the artificial head and so assists in casting.

To preserve eel-tails is quite easy. They can be kept in an extra strong solution of brine, formalin or a mixture of formalin and glycerine. Baits preserved in formalin are tainted with a smell but this can be overcome quite easily by putting the baits in brine three hours before they are needed for use. Formalin has the advantage over all other preservatives of

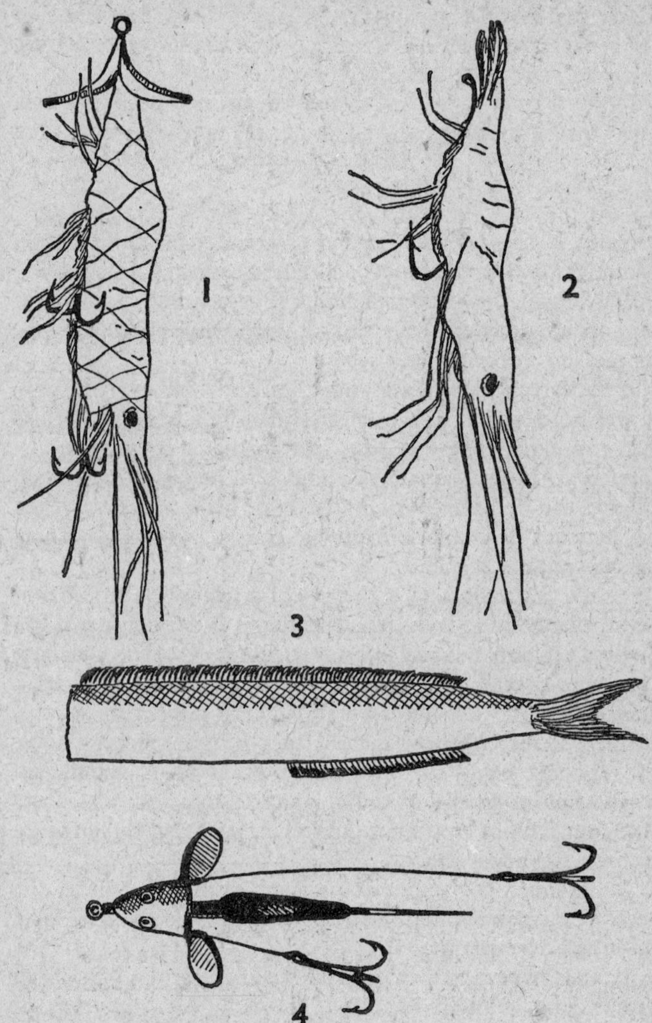

Fig. 43 Natural Baits for Spinning

1. Prawn with binding and spinner attached
2. Prawn with single hook
3. Sand-eel Tail
4. Sand-eel Tail spinner

making the eel-tails as tough as leather without harming the colour. Further, in this chemical they will last for years as long as they are kept airtight when not in use.

If you happen to be in a place where fresh sand-eels can be caught easily every day there is no need to bother with preserved baits, but it is always best to have a jar ready in case you may need an eel-tail in a hurry.

For fish that are inhabiting places far from brackish water, the gold or silver sprat will take some beating, the only trouble being that it is very soft and has to be renewed quite often. In regard to the silver (natural coloured) sprat it is an exceedingly good bait during intense cold spells, and by cold I mean those days when glycerine has to be used on the rings to prevent the line from freezing to them.

Sprats can be preserved in the same way as eel-tails and can be coloured gold quite cheaply and easily. Here's how: For a few pence a chemist will supply a solution of Acriflavine made up to a strength of 1/750 in which the little fish are soaked for at least four days; if large, allow a week. At the end of that time they will have taken on a beautiful golden colour and can then be packed and preserved in jars to await use.

With sprat and eel-tail, work the deep holes and pools paying particular attention to the rocky areas where the fish can get cover and protection from the fierce currents and heavy flow of water. Keep the bait moving, not too fast and not too slowly, trying if possible to imitate the speed of a fish if it were swimming. Experience will teach you more than mere words, but should you hook a fish try and remember the speed you were working the bait, where the bait was taken and so on and on your next cast try and copy everything you did when you had the bite.

Other natural baits for the early days are minnows and loach (a very good bait in North-East rivers) and worms.

Minnows and loach are spun the same as the sprat and over similar places. The worm is a coloured-water bait and can be deadly just after a flood. A bunch of worms is impaled on a hook and allowed to float down the stream into the quiet water of a pool. Or if there has been little movement the worms can be cast into the pool and left there for a little while to see

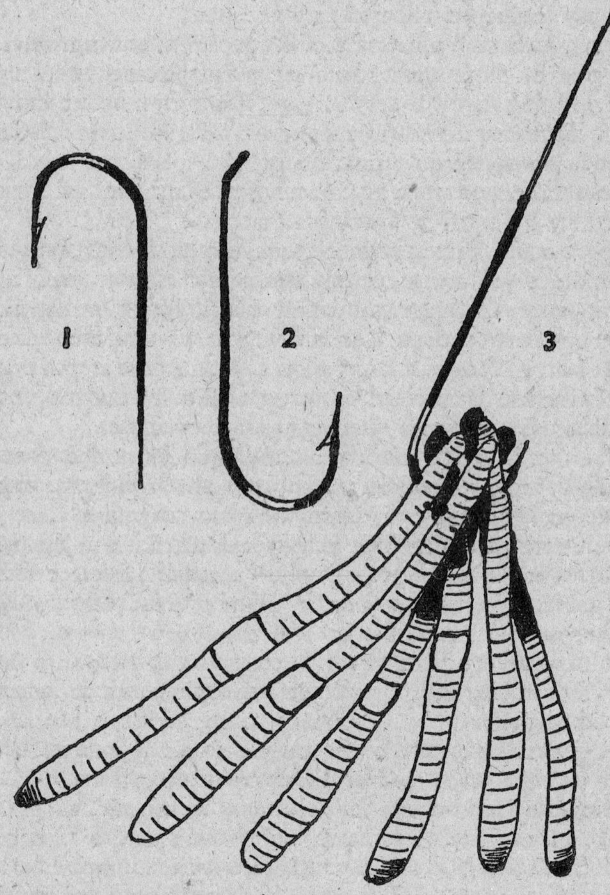

Fig. 44 Hooks for Worming
1. Round bend for whipping leader to
2. Eyed round bend
3. Whipped hook baited up

if a salmon will pick the bait up. One of my largest Welsh salmon, a fish of twenty-three pounds fell to the lure of a bunch of worms while I was taking a rest to nibble at a sandwich.

Put the worms on the hook so that the tail of each one is free to wriggle. It is this seductive movement which attracts. Round bend hooks are best for worm fishing.

May, June, July, August and September is prawn time. In the deep pools this bait can be fixed to spinning tackle and spun over the most likely looking spots. However, to my way of thinking the main beauty of the prawn is its usefulness during times of low water.

Low water prawning is down stream fishing and the angler MUST avail himself of every bit of cover. While it can be used on the spinning rod my preference is for the fly rod. Cast the prawn into the head of a stream, pay out about ten yards of line and then start working it by lifting the rod top to about thirty degrees. The bait will rise to near the surface and then fall back as you lower the rod to its original position. Every so often let out more line until there are about twenty yards off the reel. Work every inch before moving on.

Prawn tackles for this type of fishing can be purchased and once you have a pattern, it is an easy matter to make some providing you are fairly handy with a soldering iron.

I have found that it is best to use a wire trace for this tackle as it helps to keep the bait down. Always remember that in mounting a prawn the tail is at the head of the tackle, which is the reverse of other baits.

In the mounting of all kinds of natural baits take your time. Remember fish, and in particular salmon, are apt to inspect a bait many times before actually taking it. When you have the needle through the prawn and the hooks in position, take half a dozen turns around the prawn and tackle with pink cotton or nylon to ensure that the hooks stay in position.

A pint of prawns from a fishmonger will provide a couple of dozen good baits which can be preserved in brine or salt. As they are on sale during a greater part of the year a supply of fresh baits is assured, but always have a jar of preserved ones handy just in case there are no fishmongers' shops near.

28

USING ARTIFICIAL BAITS

Manufactured baits for the outwitting of salmon are legion and their numbers continue to grow year by year with the development of man's creative genius. However, there has never been and possibly never will be a bait, natural or artificial, that will catch fish day in and day out. There is one, though, that comes pretty near to such a grading – the spoon. It has been in use since fishing began and beyond a few refinements, such as scale finishes and colouring, is much the same in shape as when first invented thousands of years ago.

With the passing of the centuries it has become a number one salmon killer in many districts.

My box contains half a dozen spoons of different shapes and sizes. Its killing power lies undoubtedly in its versatility, because it can be made to spin, wobble on an erratic course and do all manner of antics. In other words it embodies the action of devons and plugs with a few others besides.

Quite a number of anglers have somehow got hold of the idea that spoon fishing is easy. You just fasten the bait to the trace swivel, cast it into the water and start turning the reel handle. On the face of it I agree it appears like that, particularly if one is watching an expert, but from experience I appreciate that just as much skill is required to handle a spoon if one expects to catch fish, as is employed by the average fly fisherman.

My favourite spoons for salmon are (1) a 2-inch Norwegian (Bergen) silver; (2) 1½-inch pearl and (3) 1¼-inch semi-scaled gold and silver.

The spoon can be used with the fly rod or spinning rod. More than once I have gone out with the fly rod and failed to connect with the feathers and tinsel, but have brought back a fish that fell to the wiles of a spoon.

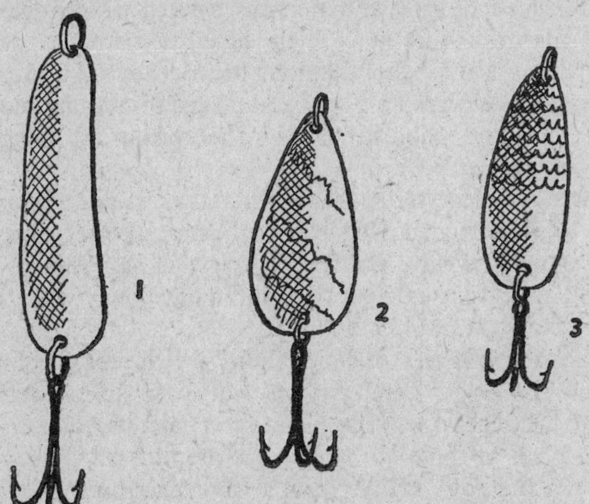

Fig. 45 Spoons for Salmon
1. 2-inch Norwegian silver Spoon
2. 1½-inch Pearl Spoon
3. 1½-inch semi-scaled Gold and Silver Spoon

Wherever there is sufficient depth of water this metal artificial should be allowed to sink well down before commencing the retrieve, and then it should be worked "sink and draw" which has already been described in a previous chapter. When you stop turning the handle, momentarily, the bait will drop downwards in a series of gyrating tumbling motions.

Cast up and across and let the current carry the spoon as far as it will before ever turning the handle. When a cast is "fished out" do not snatch the spoon from the water: this puts a heavy strain on the tip of the rod. Bring the bait to the surface and ease it up quietly, preparatory to making another cast. This is, moreover, sound fishing sense, for often salmon will follow the spoon up and take near the surface. If it is snatched away the angler spoils his chances of a strike.

Number two on my list of good all-round artificial baits is the devon. Here we have a metal bait which attracts, first by the vibration it sets up as it spins through the water on its tethered course and secondly by its flash. Fish have a very finely balanced hearing and nervous system which can pick up the slightest vibration. Their sight, however, is not so attuned and it is my belief that long before they see a spinning bait they have received vibratory notice of something moving and are, if in the mood to take, on the lookout for the cause of the disturbance.

It does not necessarily follow that the greater vibrations set up by a swiftly moving bait will attract better than one that is moving slowly. On the contrary, it has been proved time and again that a devon that is moving slowly will attract a strike much better.

In the devon series of baits there are dozens of shapes, sizes and also colour combinations, but so far science has not bettered for general use the plain silver and its counter-part in gold. Next to these my vote is for the blue and silver and the brown and gold and any angler who relies on this quartet for a spinning period will not go far wrong.

It has been my experience that grilse have a decided preference for plain silver or blue and silver and adult salmon seem to like the other pair. Autumn fish in particular, following a spate, will strike at a brown and gold to the exclusion of all other types of devons.

For coloured water the reflex (flat-sided) type throws off more light and far heavier vibrations, even when moving slowly, than the ordinary rounded devon. For loch fishing where distance reached can be an asset, its extra weight will assist in achieving this.

Where there are very wide pools, like we have on the Tweed for instance, one can use devons that have been specially constructed for such work. They are twice and sometimes three times the weight of the usual type. For the usual run of salmon pools they are not very productive in that they sink far too rapidly and tend to foul the river bed more often when retrieved slowly.

In all river devon fishing cast the same way as when using a spoon, bearing in mind the lighter in weight the line the greater the distance can be cast and the bait works much more easily.

In recent years plugs of various designs have been used for

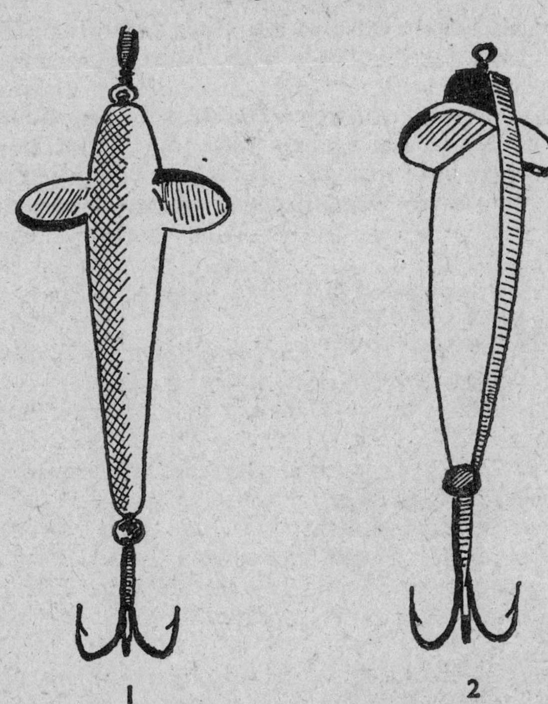

Fig. 46 Devons
1. 2-inch Gold and Brown Devon
2. 2-inch Gold Reflex Devon

salmon but this method of fishing is still, so to speak, in its infancy, old time anglers preferring to stick to the baits they know. Many years ago my wife and I fished a whole fortnight with plug baits and our total catch was three salmon, all of which fell to a plastic plug minnow. We experimented with jointed ones, divers, etc., but it was the only design that registered with the fish.

We have also had an odd fish or two on plastic flipper baits and also on a plastic and feather lure. I am not recommending such baits, for while they have been in existence many years in America they are comparatively newcomers on this side of the

Atlantic. They look attractive in the box and are worth a try now and then; beyond that I must leave the reader to please himself.

One of the best imports from America in the way of lures for salmon is without doubt the streamer flies. These can be used with either fly or spinning rod. With the fly rod they are worked in similar way to the fly proper, but with the shorter

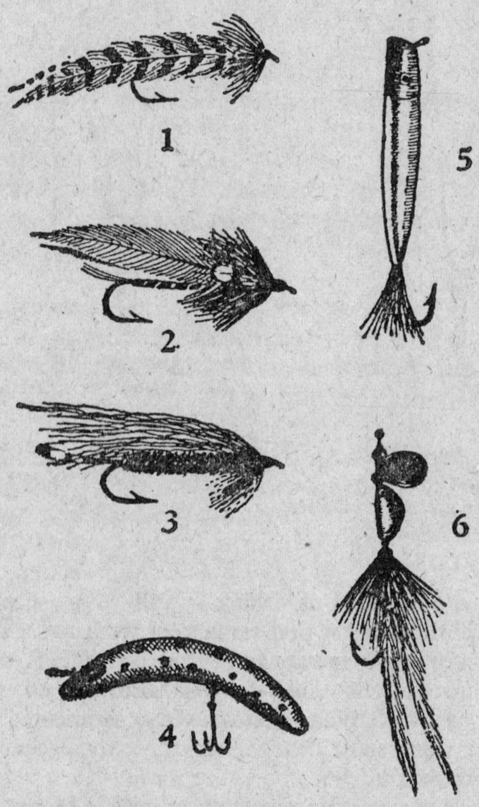

Fig. 47 Feathers, Hair and Plastic Baits for Spinning Rod

1. Grey Ghost Streamer
2. Black Ghost Streamer
3. Deer Hair Streamer
4. Flipper Bait
5. Plug minnow
6. Plastic and Feather Lure

rod one can get a greater distance and for this reason it is one of the best feather and tinsel baits to use for wide pools and lochs. An anti-kink or other small lead weight must be used to get a long cast but for small waters there is no need – the weight of the long-shanked hook upon which the lure is dressed being quite sufficient to get twenty or thirty yards.

On occasions I have used a couple of split shot near the head of the fly to get an extra couple of yards, but if you can manage without additional weight so much the better.

The value of this lure lies, not only in its fish-taking capabilities, but in the fact that it is so easy to make at home. A glance at the sketch will give you some idea as to the simplicity of its make-up.

We, my family and I, have tried all sorts of streamers and the trio in the sketch have always produced best results for us. The Grey Ghost is made up of an embossed silver body with a couple of barred Plymouth Rock cock hackles with a black and grey hackle wound at the head.

The Black Ghost (a decided favourite of mine) has a golden pheasant topping for the tail, a black floss silk body ribbed with oval silver tinsel, a couple of white hackle feathers and jungle cock at the shoulders with golden yellow hackle wound at the head.

The Deer-hair streamer is composed of a couple of jungle cock feathers, side-by-side for the tail, body green and bronze peacock herl, the hair is from the tail of a red deer and the hackle is black and guinea-fowl mixed. This pattern has proved its worth time and again among large sea trout during night fishing.

A friend of mine took a nine pound sea trout and also an eight and a half pounder in one night on this pattern. He was no expert as he had just started his game fishing career and prior to that had fished for nothing but coarse fish. Beginner's luck, maybe, but I think some credit is also due to the deer-hair streamer he was using which had been made from a red deer killed on the road from Strathcarron to Shiledaig (Scotland) when it collided with a lorry. I happened to be staying in the area at the time and managed to get hold of the tail and incidentally, a nice taste of venison.

29

FOILING THE POACHER

As the years go by, poaching, instead of becoming less, appears to be on the increase, at least that is what keepers, lessees and owners of salmon water tell me. Some keeper friends of mine blame the advance of certain sciences for this. They quote the fact that the advent of polaroid glasses gave the poacher what amounts to a weapon, against which there is no law. A poacher wearing polaroids, can, during periods of low water and sunshine see every fish in a pool and make his arrangements accordingly. Years ago the poacher netted a pool without much knowledge of how many fish were there. Today guesswork has been practically eliminated.

Then again science has brought out many poisons, which for obvious reasons I do not propose to mention here. The days of carbide and lime, etc., have passed together more or less with the gaff and light. The modern poacher, if nothing else, does keep abreast of the times and adapts certain discoveries to his nefarious operations. We have nets made of nylon that are of little weight or bulk that can lie hidden near the river for days without danger of rotting. In addition, some poachers have already seen the commercial possibilities of stunning fish with electricity, a method which originated, like polaroids and nylon, in America. However, in many parts of the British Isles the net is still operated by poaching gangs and this coupled with a spotter or two who are armed with polaroid glasses can be a deadly combination on any stretch of water. As the law stands, providing there is no trespass, no one can prevent a man walking along the bank of a river wearing sunglasses. After all, this particular type of glasses are sold as protection for the eyes against the sun.

A dry summer which reduces most rivers to mere trickles of their former selves plays right into the hands of such individuals, for the pools become gin-clear. Under such conditions illegal netsmen can do untold harm to the future production of any particular water they attack. The old method of driving into the bed of the river steel stakes is of little use as these are fairly easily removed by the poachers before the net is used.

However, while I was fishing the river Urr, Dalbeattie, Scotland, many years ago, was shown a device which has put an end to netting on that part of the river controlled by the Dalbeattie Angler's Association. Previous to its introduction the Urr had been poached severely until it was reduced to one salmon run and that very late in the season. Today, there is a splendid spring run, a late summer invasion and the usual autumn run.

The man who had been largely responsible for bringing back early salmon to this river was the local association secretary Mr. D. Forbes Strachan. It was he who invented the giant "Treble" which has proved the death knell of the poaching netsmen.

On the banks of the Urr at Dalbeattie is a world famous granite quarry and from there Mr. Strachan obtained large rounded blocks of granite, each weighing several hundredweight. The local blacksmith created from two inch steel bars the giant treble complete with barbs; these were embedded and fixed into the granite. When a number had been made, they were lowered by means of block and tackle into the various holding pools, three, four and five to a pool. With their advent poaching with the net came to an end, but it took the river several years to get back to normal, so serious had been the inroads made in the salmon population.

Speaking to me, Mr. Strachan held the view that if this method was adopted the illegal netsmen would have a very lean time. "Of course, we have complaints occasionally from anglers who have lost a salmon when the line fouls a 'treble' but by and large very few fish are lost. For my part, I would rather hear of one fish being lost than have a report that a pool had been netted."

Another important point about the River Urr is that it is well keepered, despite the fact that there is only one part-time keeper. Every angler is a keeper and woe betide the man

Fig. 48 A "Forbes Strachan" Netting Spoiler

who does anything that is not in keeping with the rules and general sportsmanship. The local police also work in close liaison with the Association.

Let me illustrate what I mean. A flood during late June of 1955 brought a number of salmon and sea trout into the burn which flows through Dalbeattie. They settled in the Bridge Pool and for the fortnight they were in residence there, the police kept a careful watch to see that no illegal methods were used to affect their capture. With such co-operation is it any wonder that the Urr is now a good river to fish both the fly rod and spinners? Would that other rivers were as good.

I have been amazed in recent years by attempts which have been made to invest fish poachers with a degree of romance – on stage, screen and in our literature. The truth, however, is that they are a good-for-nothing, idly disposed set of rascals who differ little from habitual thieves and the people who purchase such fish at greatly reduced prices are infinitely worse, for without receivers there would be few commercial poachers. In Scotland and certain parts of England, Wales and Ireland large sums of money change hands every year for poached salmon and sea trout.

Frankly, it is my belief that if each and every angler kept a lookout for individuals acting suspiciously and when such are encountered advised the bailiff or a policeman, we should be well on the way to a solution to this age old problem. Any reticence on the part of legitimate anglers to act as I suggest is a direct assistance to those who spoil their sport for gain. Only by every angler becoming an unpaid bailiff can we hope to put an end to poaching.

The method adopted by the Dalbeattie Angler's Association will end netting. Of that I am convinced. But only keen observation will clear from our rivers the poisoners, dynamite operators, and those who use snares and gaff. The poacher, like pollution, is an arch-enemy of good-fishing and should be treated as such whenever met. It must be obvious to everyone who loves to fish that Nature unaided is powerless in the task of repopulating our waters. It is up to all of us to help her and in the course of time she will repay with better and bigger runs of fish.

30

COOKING THE CATCH

Having caught your salmon, what is the best way to cook it? Should it be boiled, steamed, fried, baked or grilled? In most cookery books there are excellent recipes but those appended here are the best my wife and I have tried. At the outset let me say this. A salmon cooked within a few hours of being caught is always better flavoured than one that has been kept on ice for several days.

Immediately a salmon is landed it should be killed by a sharp blow on the head. This shock to the nervous system results in the muscular tissue of the fish becoming rigid and firm. A fish that is not killed outright and allowed to die from strangulation becomes soft and is not so good to eat.

For some years now my family's favourite dish from the first salmon caught is steaks covered in oatmeal and fried in deep fat. As a matter of fact we have been doing this for so many years now that it has become something of an annual ritual. But to get the utmost flavour it must be fried the same day as it is caught. A steak from a freshly caught salmon takes some beating.

Another easy way is to steam portions of four or five pounds in weight. In the old days my wife used the ordinary method of a pan of boiling water with another pan on top, the bottom of which was a collander which allowed the steam to get through. The juice of the fish which drops into the water is used to make a wine sauce from cheap sherry. The steaming process takes about forty minutes. With the wine sauce the fish is served with finely chopped parsley, when cold, and makes a nice basis for a salad. Today we use a pressure cooker, which is just as good.

In boiling a salmon, whether whole or in part, add one dessertspoonful of salt to every quart of water. This will ensure that the curd remains between the flakes of flesh. Forget the salt and your prized curd, which is largely composed of albumin as in the white of a hen's egg, will dissolve in the water. Let the fish simmer and allow ten minutes per pound. It is ready when the flesh is easily removed from the bones. As a garnish one can have ordinary parsley sauce or shrimp hollandaise. Plain melted butter is also nice for a change. It should be served with new potatoes and fresh garden peas.

A most popular dish is salmon mayonnaise. A piece three pounds in weight which has been boiled or steamed and allowed to go cold, is cut into convenient pieces for serving. The crisp hearts of two or three lettuce, thick mayonnaise, sliced cucumber and beetroot with a couple of hard-boiled eggs are the ingredients for this tasty dish.

A couple of years ago my wife and I had our first taste of broiled salmon, and I might mention we have had a similar dish many times since. Our initiation took place in an Inverness (Scotland) hotel and we so enjoyed it that we asked the chef for the recipe. Here it is: Cut some steaks to suit your appetite and melt about three tablespoons of butter to which has been added a little salt and pepper. Put the fish under a heated grill and cook for about eight or ten minutes when the steaks will have turned a nice golden brown. During the grilling brush the fat on at least three or four times. When one side is browned turn over and repeat. Serve with parsley sauce to which a little white wine has been added.

So much for salmon. Large sea trout can be cooked the same way as salmon, but the little chaps of only half a pound to a pound are best fried. From a pound to three pounds in weight fillet and fry. But I repeat, the sooner you cook your catch the better you will enjoy it. If you cannot use it all then by all means give a cutlet or two to your friends.

Every year when I have a slice or two to spare my practice is to give some to poultry and game bird dealer friends and in return they keep me supplied with feathers for making flies. It is also a nice gesture to give the river bailiff a cutlet. Many a time such an investment has returned good dividends in my being shown a particularly good lie and also in being given assistance when it was sorely needed.

I recall one such instance which took place on the Coquet (Northumberland). I was fishing a place known as the Gut. It is full of rocks and while salmon are fairly easy to land, at times there are occasions when a companion comes in handy. On this particular day I had hooked a lively fish on a Brown Turkey fly. Everything was coming along nicely when the fish decided to explore the other side of the river, and there was nothing I could do about it. Needless to say the river was running heavy and tree branches and debris of all kinds was coming down. A large branch entangled the line and the fish went under a tree root just to make things a little more awkward.

Just as I was about to give up the struggle and let the fish keep the fly, along came a bailiff. He saw at a moment that predicament I was in and hurried up the river with my gaff. Crossing over to the other side (I don't know to this day how he managed it) he released the line from the branch, got the fish from out of the roots, then came back and a few minutes later gaffed it for me, a clean fish of 9¼ lb. It gave me great pleasure when he accepted half of that fish for he had earned it.

Today any angler can enjoy that most delicious of foods – smoked salmon, by simply purchasing for a few pounds a smoking outfit from his tackle dealer. As mentioned in an earlier chapter, oak sawdust is the best kind to use. Fillet your fish and cut into pieces to fit your smoker and in a very short time you have some good meals at hand. If you have a deep-freeze unit you can keep smoked salmon for months, and the beauty of prior cutting into pieces assists in that you can take out one or two without thawing the rest. Once you have defrosted fish it is not safe to replace it in the deep freeze as it may become tainted and unsafe to eat.

31

NATURAL HISTORY OF SEA TROUT

Here is a fish I never tire of talking about. It is one of Nature's finest examples of streamlining and inside its small but well-shaped head is a brain capable of setting many tests for the angler. On the question of gameness it is the equal of anything that swims. Bold words, maybe, but they are backed by years of experience with this splendid breed. Unlike a salmon, which often sulks after its first break for freedom, a sea trout will fight to the last. I have yet to meet a sea trout that included sulkiness in its repertoire. When the barb goes home this ocean-loving trout generally jumps into top gear and tries to put as much distance between the angler as possible and in so doing takes to the air in flashing leaps as many times as strength will allow.

While I enjoy a day's salmon fishing, if given a choice mine would be sea trout every time. The salmon, in my opinion, so far as courage and gameness is concerned, is a much over-rated fish. Invariably the salmon has pounds extra in weight to help in its fight for freedom, whereas the sea trout, with few exceptions, has only speed and a fighting heart. I appreciate that the tackle used for sea trout is much lighter, but even when a pound fish is hooked on salmon tackle he will put up a very fine show. If the salmon is king then the sea trout is the prince of freshwater.

The spawning period of sea trout is usually from October to December and takes place in burns and streams that are tributaries of the main river. The eggs take about ninety days to hatch out. It is a well-known fact that this species never wanders far from the estuary of the river which saw its birth. It enters the sea between two and three years old. On quite a few occasions sea trout that have been "tagged" in one river have been caught in another some miles distant, which leads

Fig. 49 Sea Trout

one to suppose that the homing instinct of the salmon is more pronounced than in its relative, the sea trout.

It is a fish with many different names. In the West Country – Devon and Cornwall – it is called peal, in Wales sewin, Ireland it is widely referred to as white trout and in Scotland on its first run into fresh water it is known as whitling, herling, finnock, or black nebs, depending on the locality.

The first time I heard the term "black neb" used was on Loch Lomond. My wife and I had been on holiday for three weeks and had done practically nothing, then we had a flood and the following day we caught, between us, nine one-pound sea trout. We were admiring our catch when another angler stopped to pass the time of day and surprised us by saying "I see the black nebs have been biting".

Some rivers have been known to have a spring run, but by

Fig. 50 River Lies of Sea Trout
1. Flat water between rocks
2. Streamy water below falls
3. At the tails of pools

and large the angler who has set his mind on catching sea trout should fix up his holidays between the second week in June and the first week in September. Whereas the salmon waits for a flood to enter a river, a sea trout will leave the estuary as soon as the temperature is right. Its preference is for warm weather and while most of its travelling in fresh water is done at night it detests moonlight.

Night Fishing for sea trout is a fetish of mine, but so far I have yet to take a sea trout when the moon was full. The rays of Luna are not conducive to good fishing so when contemplating a night's fishing bear in mind the phases of the moon. Some of my best takes at night have been when there has been no moon or when it has been in its first phase. Why sea trout should be so affected I have never found out, but quite a few scientists state that certain other species of fish are also rendered dormant when the moon is full.

In every sea trout water the biggest shoals will be found in those areas where there is plenty of streamy as well as flat water, with a pool over-shadowed with bushes and trees here and there for cover.

It is more wary than even a river trout so the angler should take advantage of every bit of cover available during day-time fishing, and at night should stand as far away from the water's edge as possible.

In lochs the sea trout favours sandy and shingle bays, shaded shallow water and near the mouths of feeder streams up which it will run for spawning when conditions are right.

Certain localities breed larger fish than others. In Devon and Cornwall the average is from a pound to three pounds with an occasional fish of nine or ten pounds.

A friend of mine who for twenty years owned a stretch of the Tavy once told me that the fish ran in cycles of four years. For three years the fish would be averaging one to two-and-a-half pounds, and the fourth year would see a run of very big sea trout – fish of eight to twelve pounds.

In Wales where I fished as a boy, youth and young man there were lean periods for two or three years then there would be shoals of good fish. In Ireland the average is just over a pound. In the Lowlands of Scotland and North of England there is a

Fig. 51 Loch Lomond This famous beauty spot is well-known for its Sea Trout fishing. There are similar lies in most lochs. 1. & 2. Sandy and shingle bays 3. Near the mouths of feeder streams 4. Shaded shallow water

periodic run of big fish, but in many parts of the Highlands, particularly on the West Coast, the shoals appear to be fairly evened out each year with fish of five and six pounds always present. In Finland and Norway, which I fished quite a lot at one time, there were also periodic runs of good sea trout.

The inference to be drawn from these facts is that while hundreds of sea trout enter freshwater after about twelve months in salt water as whitling, herling, etc., quite a large number remain feeding in the sea for two or three years before returning to a river. Very often large numbers of sea trout of four and five pounds are taken in the coastal and estuary nets, but not one fish is recorded on rod and line over two pounds. From this it would appear that the big fellows work in and out with the tide for a year or two before attempting to run.

32

FLY-FISHING FOR SEA TROUT

The fly patterns for sea trout in rivers are nearly as numerous as those for ordinary trout, but there is a big difference in the dressing. The flies for trout are very often sombre-hued while those for sea trout, nine times out of ten, have plenty of colour and tinsel. In the sketch are illustrations of sixteen of the more famous flies, patterns that are known as killers throughout the whole of the British Isles. Each year, in the light of further knowledge of this fly question, I change my opinion as to the qualifications of one fly over another, but the twelve patterns I started out with (not the flies!) still find a place in my box. One season it will be one particular fly that will take best and another season it will be something else. Wherever I go my faith is pinned on those twelve. Like scores of other anglers I have experimented with many types of flies, but my first loves remain the same. Here they are: Teal and Black, Butcher, Teal and Green, Silver March Brown, Cinnamon and Gold, Black and Green, Grouse and Claret, Mallard and Claret, Alexandra, Peter Ross, Blue Kingfisher and Blue Zulu.

Temperature of the water determines the comfort of all fish and the sea trout is no exception. Water that is too cold numbs the sea trout and they stop feeding. Water that is too hot makes them lethargic. That is why a good sea trout place is where a fast rock-strewn stream feeds a deep pool.

Abundance of food is a second prime factor. They love minnows and underwater insect life, therefore the first thing to do on a strange water, and I repeat what has already been said earlier on and make no apology for so doing, is to study the water. Those places which appear to be the most likely food-producing areas should be fished carefully, paying the utmost attention to fairly deep streams and flats which usually start at the heads and tails of pools.

13 14 15 16

Fig. 52 Sea Trout Flies and Spiders

1. Teal and Black
2. Butcher
3. Teal and Green
4. Silver March Brown
5. Cinnamon and Gold
6. Black and Green
7. Grouse and Claret
8. Mallard and Claret
9. Alexandra
10. Blue Kingfisher
11. Peter Ross
12. Blue Jay
13. Red Palmer
14. Black Zulu
15. Blue Zulu
16. March Brown

Most fly-fishing is with the wet-fly, and it is essential to get the flies down to the fish, which during the hours of daylight usually lie deep. In the swift water generally used by them, the usual method of casting across the current and letting the flies swing round and below the angler may result in their passing too far above the fish to be seen.

Here is where the dry-fly angler's trick of reducing line drag may be used to good advantage to sink the cast deeper. The cast is made up stream and across, and extra line is pulled from the reel and fed out through the rings to help the line belly sink and carry the flies deeper before the current seizes the leader.

The fast-striking sea trout is difficult to hook on the loose line, before it is finally straightened out, but the speed with which it usually comes at the fly repeatedly proves its undoing, at least I have found it so when fishing fast-flowing streams and pools. Nylon tapered leaders of two to three pounds are excellent for fish up to three pounds, but if the water is known to contain some bigger ones use a much stronger leader.

If you can avoid wading do so, more good fishing has been spoiled by indiscriminate wading than anything else. If you don't study your own fishing at least give a thought to the chap who might be following you.

In Scotland most of the local anglers use a three fly leader, but my preference is for two during daylight and one at night. Three flies may be all right on a loch but in a river the least number of flies "running loose" the better. Even a leader with a couple of flies can prove a menace if there are weed beds and other obstructions about. I have more than once lost a fish through the other fly becoming snagged.

Ordinary trout fly tackle is all right providing the reel holds, including thirty yards doubled tapered line, sixty yards in all. If one is to fish regularly water containing heavy fish then it is far better to invest in a sea trout fly rod and reel, for invariably where you have sea trout there you will have a salmon or two. Salmon and heavy sea trout have been killed on trout gear, but the rod takes an awful beating and usually ends up with a nasty "set" in the top joint if it is split cane.

The dry-fly is not a usual lure of sea trout but on occasions when there is a heavy hatch of large night flies one might take an odd fish or two with a "floater". The patterns most suitable for this are Red Palmer, Black Palmer, and a palmered Cinnamon and Gold.

A friend of mine who fishes a Welsh stream reckons to catch a score or more on the dry-fly each season, his biggest baskets being at night during July and August. However, the angler who sticks to wet-flies will not go far wrong.

If the water is low, which is generally the case during the sea trout season, try the sea trout size flies first and if there are no takers switch over to trout sizes of the same patterns. A change in size of pattern is often better than a change of fly.

On occasions when using a nymph for river trout a sea trout has taken, but many times the nymph has been fished religiously without a bite, so, like the dry-fly the nymph is classed by me as an occasional lure to be tried when all else has failed, a sort of do-or-die effort. If the fish are in a taking mood you will catch them on one of the patterns mentioned. If not, at least you will have had a nice taste of fresh air among pleasant surroundings. What is more, you will have realised that there is more in fishing than just being able to cast a good fly.

33

THE FLY AT NIGHT

It is obvious that to be successful with fly at night one should be well acquainted with the water to be fished. It is simply asking for trouble to go on to a strange water without first studying it during the daytime, memorising the best places for fishing and likely spots for landing a big fish, for at night your chance of hooking a specimen is much greater as large fish do most of their feeding after dark.

Fishing at night is just like fishing in the daytime except that you handle your tackle by touch alone and the fish move into different waters. Instead of the pools, flats and very rough water they now frequent the shallow streams, feeding on minnows and the fry of trout. To avoid entanglements in the leader use *only one fly*. A flash-light is a necessity, but do not wave it around any more than you have to. So far as I am aware any pattern that will catch fish in the daytime will work at night, but bearing in mind that the sea trout are after fish food there is a series of flies which imitate the actions of minnows and other small fish. I refer to the demons and terrors of which there are many patterns. The half-dozen in the sketch are the best my family and I have tried so far and are placed in order of merit based on the kills made over the last twenty-five years.

With this type of fly the secret is to keep it on the move so that it is working just below the surface or about mid-water. You will have to learn the art of "shooting a line" after working the fly close and collecting the slack by hand. A double-tapered line is much better for shooting than a level one. It is just a question of timing that practice alone can give. With several yards of line held in the hand the cast is made and just as the pull of the line is exerting pressure on the rod top the line held in the hand is released and the forward pull of the

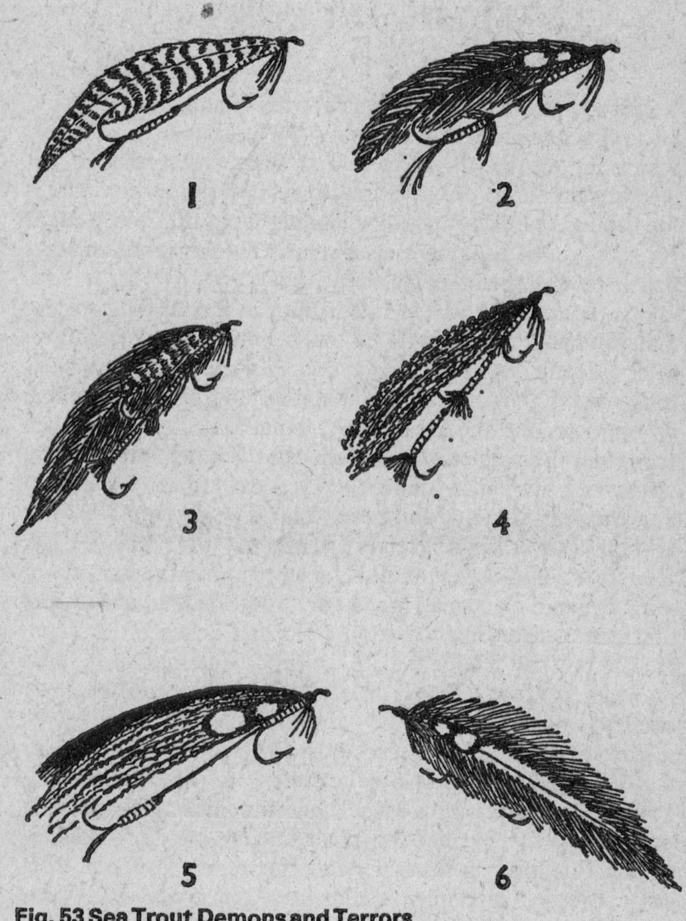

Fig. 53 Sea Trout Demons and Terrors

1. Teal and Silver
2. Blue and Silver
3. Mallard and Blue
4. Peacock and Silver
5. Alexandra and Jungle
6. Blue Elver

cast brings it through the guides. Very long casts can be made with this method even if you are standing among trees or bushes.

On the Ythan, a famous sea trout river of Scotland, the terrors used are real giants ranging from 2½ inches to 3½ inches. However, in practice, I have found 1½ to 2 inches are ideal sizes to handle on a fly rod.

They are a little more costly to buy than ordinary flies, but once you have a pattern are very easy to make.

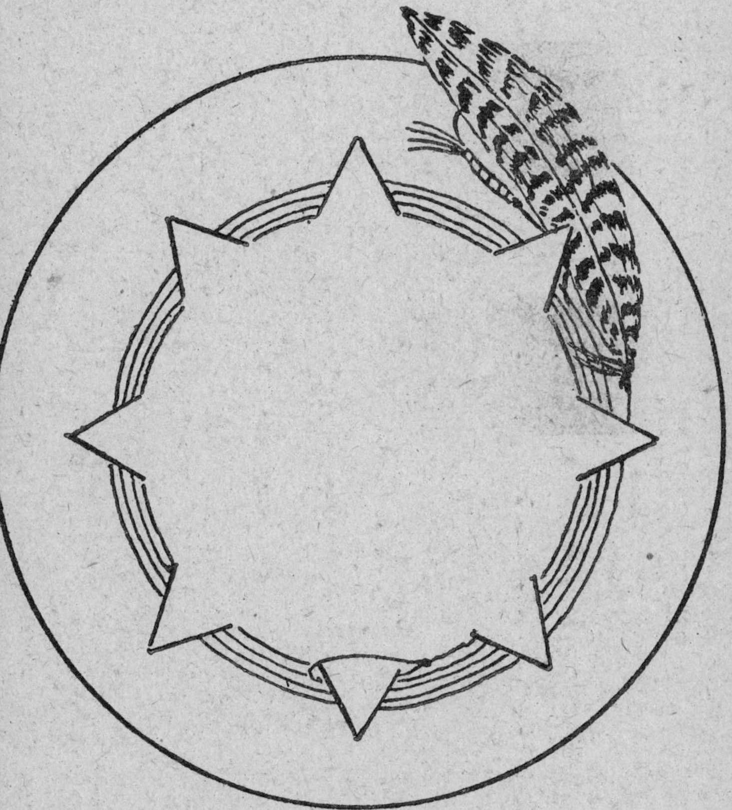

Fig. 54 Leader-Holder for Night Fishing

Incidentally, it is always best to have at least three leaders mounted (fly attached) and wound on to a leader-holder of cardboard or celluloid. The one illustrated is of the latter material.

All you need to make the holder is a compass and a pair of scissors, with a razor blade to cut the Vs around which the leader is wound. Do a couple in cardboard first and then when you have the idea make them of celluloid as it is more serviceable and not affected by damp.

34

ESTUARY FISHING

The best of all places to fish for sea trout is an estuary and until you have hooked and played an estuary fish you have not, in my opinion, experienced the cream of fishing for him. A clean salmon is often likened to a "bar of living silver", but if anything a sea trout taken from salt or brackish water is more brilliantly adorned, particularly during the month of June.

It is an interesting fact that sea trout in estuaries rise to a fly more freely than when they are in fresh water and indeed call for less skill in their capture.

Fishing a Scottish Highland estuary some years ago I had as a companion a well-known London roach angler, whose knowledge of fly-fishing was what he had gleaned from watching me on a Hertfordshire stream. On his first outing on that estuary he took six lovely sea trout, the largest of which weighed two pounds. This, he thought, went to show that fly-fishing for sea trout in estuary water is not difficult. As we packed up he remarked: "Well, if that's sea trout fishing it is much easier than catching roach".

I mention the incident for one thing, to illustrate the difference in the two kinds of fishing. On the river one had to take advantage of cover and be as careful as possible not to alarm the fish. In tidal water the sea trout is not so wary for I could quote many instances where novices have had good bags from estuaries.

I have never found the brightly-coloured flies of river fishing to be very effective in or near salt water, and have carried out numerous experiments with various colour combinations. For this style of fishing I now use only one pattern which was evolved as a direct result of my tests and trials. This fly has neither tail nor hackle, the wings are dull black, and the body is dressed with flat silver tinsel. I make them up in two sizes, No. 12 for places where four or five pound fish are known to frequent and No. 14 for small estuaries. The wings can be made from ordinary feathers or hackles. See illustration.

Fig. 55 The Author's Black Fly
1. Made with ordinary feather 2. Made from tips of Hackle feathers

Knowing the state of the tide has a lot to do with the success or otherwise of a day's fishing. When the tide is at half ebb or half flow has usually given me good sport, and the first two pools from the sea are those upon which the angler should concentrate, especially in localities where there are plenty of seaweed-covered rocks. I have often seen the flash from silvery sides as the fish foraged among the weeds in places of this sort.

On a bright sunny day one or other of the demons or terrors mentioned can be tried with a fair hope of success. However, I always stick to the black fly for this reason. Open up the first fish you take in an estuary and you will find its stomach containing small fish fry with the main colour combination of black and silver. When the black fly is moving in the water it has the appearance of a very small fish. It has also taken a few salmon. On the River Urr a couple of seasons ago I gave a fly to a friend who, whilst fishing a pool adjoining the tidal stretch, hooked and landed a nine pound fresh run salmon on it. He had originally been fishing for sea trout.

When the tide is nearly full, float tackle and a No. 12 hook baited with a small, freshly caught prawn will sometimes take a fish or two. A sand-eel two or three inches long is very good when estuary fishing on a flood tide at night, providing sand-eels frequent the locality. It should be used alive, hooked in the back and allowed to move back and forth with the tide, in channels between rocks and weeds.

For the spinning enthusiast wide pools with few obstacles are the ideal spots, but use very small silver or blue and silver devons. Most of my estuary devons measure only half an inch, excluding hook.

As to suitable rods and reels, if you have a nine foot trout fly rod and reel and a trout spinning rod and reel you are ideally equipped and could wish for nothing better. I would, however, remind my reader that sea-water is no friend of fresh-water fishing tackle, and precautions for its protection must be taken both before and after its use in either sea or brackish water.

Before setting out give the rod a good rub over with wax polish, and a rub with an oily rag will prevent your reel corroding. On your return from fishing, even if you are tired out, take the line off the reel and give it a good wash in cold water, after which wind it on to a line-dryer and leave it there overnight. The reel should be dismantled, cleaned thoroughly and given a good oiling before it is put away. This may sound fussy, but it will save you pounds. Even nylon fly lines, while not affected by damp, can be injured by salt crystals if they are allowed to dry in. With sea water prevention is always better than cure.

If you have been fishing at night go over your flies and leaders carefully. It is amazing how many barbs of flies can be knocked off or bent over.

I recall one night my son hooked a couple of sea trout one after the other only to lose them after their first run. He changed his fly and eventually ended the night with three fish. Returning to the hotel we checked the suspect fly and sure enough the barb was missing. A check of the leaders will very often reveal that some of them have been badly frayed on the sharp rocks. Nylon is cheap enough so burn such leaders and use new. It is far better to be sure of a leader than sorry afterwards.

To conclude this chapter, I should hate it to be thought that I catch fish on every outing. I take a few like most other estuary anglers, but there are days and nights when nothing at all results from hours of fishing. These are the occasions I remember far better than those which gave me a good bag. They are the occasions when skill and knowledge counts for nought against the wisdom of Nature.

35

WORM FISHING

Worming for sea trout is very similar to worming for river trout and the best chance of success will be to let the worm travel along the bed of the stream at just the pace of the current. The cast is made up and across the spot selected, with the angler keeping well out of sight. One worm is used as bait. It should have undergone a toughening-up process at least three days before use. This is easily achieved by placing the worms in a box three parts filled with moss. At the end of three days the worms have got rid of most of the body fat and are lively and tough. A worm that is used shortly after it has been dug out of the ground or a manure heap is very soft and often breaks when casting.

Two or three inches is an ideal length for a bait and this is impaled near the head on a No. 8 or No. 10 round bend hook. There is no need to bury the hook inside the worm as so many anglers seem to think. You don't hide the hook bend and barb when fly fishing or spinning, so why do it when using the worm? The theory that the fish sees the hook and is frightened away is not based on fact.

You can use fly rod and reel or your short rod and spinning reel. If the latter, a line of four pounds B.S. is ample, but if salmon are known to be present use your salmon spinning line to be on the safe side, because although one normally uses a bunch of worms for salmon, many have been taken on a single bait.

Every stream and eddy should be tested before moving on to the next likely spot. Early morning, dusk and at night are the three best periods.

If the water is running very fast put on a couple of split shot a foot above the worm to keep the bait on the bottom, but don't put so much weight on that the worm is more or less

Fig. 56 The Right Way with Worm

anchored. A sea trout might pick it up, but the chances are that he will pass it by and go for something that is moving naturally.

A water that is fining down after a flood is good for the worm as well as the fly. If the fly fails to connect, the worm should be tried fishing the streams and runs and paying particular attention to the eddies near under-cut banks.

Always hold about a yard of slack line in the hand so that if you get a bite you can release it without the fish feeling the pressure of taking line off the reel. When you feel a tug, tighten the line by raising the rod top, and your fish should be hooked. Always try and lead (a difficult job sometimes) a hooked fish away from the spot where he took hold so as not to scare his mates, for where there is one there will be others. Nothing will frighten a shoal more than having one of their number dashing here and there and all over the place in an unnatural manner. Try and get him as far downstream as possible before using the net. I know it sounds very easy, and it can be if sufficient care and time are taken by the angler.

Another word of warning: see that your net is large enough to handle a four or five pound fish. I well remember a day in Ireland when I was called upon to net a four pound sea trout for a visitor. His net was about the smallest I have ever seen and must have been a converted coarse fish net for it had plenty of depth but the mouth, while capable of handling a pound trout was useless for anything very much bigger.

36

THE MYSTERIOUS BULL TROUT

Quite often in the past I have listened with interest to angling colleagues relating stories of how they were "broken" by giant trout when fishing for sea trout. Most of the incidents took place either in the West of England, the North East or Scotland.

In nine cases out of ten it would appear from the evidence that the fish was neither brown nor Loch Leven trout, but a bull trout (*Salmo eriox*), round tail or "bully" as it is often called in Northumberland.

For many years I have made a close study of this great migratory trout. While many thousands of words have been written on the salmon, sea trout and trout, very little has been devoted to the bull trout. Even today, in this enlightened age, the fish is shrouded in mystery.

Many anglers in the North East and also Scotland believe that the bull trout originated from river brown trout that went to the sea and that over the centuries a new species evolved. From my investigations I am inclined a little to this theory myself. Their physical appearance and characteristics have already been dealt with in a previous chapter.

They are found in most rivers on the North East coast with particular large autumn runs in the Coquet and Tweed and also on the west coast of Scotland. I have also taken them when night fishing for sea trout in certain Devonshire rivers.

Late August and September are the best times to go after them, and as they are very powerful fish, salmon tackle is best. In late evening my wife and I have had reasonable sport when using streamer flies, but the best fish have usually fallen to the spoon or golden devon. The last named artificial is exceedingly good when daylight is merging into night, for it is then that bull trout, like brown trout, do most of their feeding.

Fig. 57 Pauperhaugh Bridge Pool
(River Coquet, Northumberland)
Famous for Sea Trout and Bull Trout

In a water which bull trout frequent they will always be found among the shoals of late run sea trout with whom they seem to get on quite well. Perhaps this fact that they move around with the more streamlined sea trout led to their being called sea trout. Be that as it may, it is one of the gamest of fish, and should you hook one give him plenty of time and wait for the signs of exhaustion before attempting to use the gaff or net.

When after these giant trout with spinning baits use a wire trace as their teeth are quite capable of severing nylon, as I have learnt to my cost.

In coloured water following a flood a natural minnow or Crocodile spinning tackle is very deadly and on a number of occasions when this combination has been used my luck has been in and a bull trout has been landed as a result.

They love broken water and their powerful shoulders and thick tail enable them to withstand very strong currents, which adds materially to the difficulty of landing a good one.

In estuary pools, which they visit when the tide is in, the eel-tail bait is deadly at night. Mounting the eel-tail has been described in the chapter on bait fishing for salmon.

This sea-loving trout is no friend of the salmon and in clear water with the aid of polaroids I have watched these "bullies" chase the salmon round and round until the so-called "king of the game fish" has sought refuge in a hole under the bank or a bed of weeds. They are definitely not an asset in salmon water.

As far back as 1880 Frank Buckland, the then chief-inspector of Her Majesty's fisheries, in his book the "Natural History of British Fishes" wrote that steps should be taken to counteract the great predominance of the bull trout over salmon. Previous to that Buckland had carried out investigation on many rivers where the bull trout flourished and he was of the opinion that as these great trout grew in numbers so the runs of salmon would deteriorate.

In his official report on the death of many salmon from disease in the River Tweed during September 1880 Frank Buckland wrote: "The superabundance of bull trout in the

Tweed is, in my opinion, one of the great causes of the salmon disease in that river."

What is the position today? As I view it very little has been done to counteract the bull trout menace, and this is no doubt due to the fact that certain people still believe the "bully" is a sea trout. I know for a fact that certain rivers that enjoyed a fairly good late summer and also an autumn run of salmon are but shadows of their former selves. Pools are full of bull trout and very few salmon are seen, let alone caught.

Water authorities could do a lot towards alleviating the problem by lengthening the netting season or allowing an open season or two on this species for anglers. Regulations could be framed to safeguard the well-being of salmon. Surely it is not beyond the ingenuity of these official bodies to frame such rules?

37

INEXPENSIVE FISHING FOR YOUR HOLIDAY

The cheapest water I know for a good fishing holiday is the River Urr (Kircudbrightshire), Scotland, where a fortnight costs only a few pounds for salmon, sea trout, bull trout and river trout. This particular stretch referred to is controlled by the Dalbeattie Angling Association and extends for about four miles – a good mile being tidal. There is plenty of excellent accommodation in Dalbeattie. Night fishing is allowed and visitors are given every assistance by local anglers.

Adjoining the Dalbeattie section is the Castle Douglas stretch of ten miles with a number of good salmon pools in its length. The Urr has a very big run of herling (young sea trout) and also large sea trout, usually from the last week in July, with other runs right to the middle of September. The autumn run of salmon is good.

Around Dumfries there is also some reasonably-priced fishing on the River Nith.

At Grantown-on-Spey the local association has several miles of good water at a reasonable price.

In Northumberland the River Coquet is a good sea trout and bull trout river but the salmon run is often late. The Coquet has always been a favourite of mine for trout fishing during April, May and early June.

In Devon, a good fortnight's fishing on the Tavy and Walkham and several other tributaries of the River Tamar, can be had at small cost. Night fishing for sea trout is permitted, but wading is prohibited, as the streams are not very wide and are easily covered. Licences are issued by the area water authorities and also local associations.

In North Wales there are numerous associations, the average

cost for a fortnight's salmon and sea trout fishing being very reasonable.

The salmon and sea trout in North Wales do not run so large as other parts of the British Isles but they are just as game. However, the same types of flies, baits and tackles can be used.

In Ireland, which I have visited on numerous occasions, the cost is very cheap for a whole season of salmon, sea trout and trout fishing. Much of the best water is leased for high prices. There are, however, quite a lot of places where there is free fishing and a letter sent to the Department of Agriculture and Fisheries, Dublin, will bring a quick reply giving the list of free waters and the best centres to stay. For anyone looking for a good-all-round fishing holiday Ireland will take some beating. Together with salmon, sea trout and trout there is also plenty of coarse fishing which, in the majority of places, is free. You do not need a licence to coarse fish and permits are easy to come by from landowners who are often glad to have pike, perch and bream removed from their waters.

In a book of this kind it is an impossibility, for reasons of space, to give all the fishing centres in the British Isles. The few mentioned are among the best and cheapest that I have tried.

If one is interested in visiting a particular place and is desirous of finding out whether there is an angling association there, a letter to the Town Clerk or Clerk to the Council will usually bring the required information, but always enclose a stamped, addressed envelope. Local authorities are always anxious to boost their particular areas, and will go to a great deal of trouble to assist a would-be visitor, at least that has always been my experience. A local newspaper office is another place where valuable information can be obtained regarding the fishing in that area. There is no need for anyone to visit a place on chance for there are so many ways in which one can get the necessary information.

38

ODDS AND ENDS

The angler need never be bored with having time on his hands for there is always plenty to do, both during the close and also the fishing season. If he is handy with tools he can make quite a lot of his own tackle.

The wise angler always cleans his tackle after a day's fishing and checks everything to see that no damage has been done. Good angling always starts hours before the water is reached by the angler seeing that his equipment is in first class order.

Devons, once you have the pattern, are fairly easy to make from brass and copper tubing, purchased from ironmongers. A silver devon is made by tinning over copper with solder. Lightweight devons of aluminium can be made from rods of that material which are fairly cheap to buy.

Sheet brass and copper of varying thicknesses can be bought to make spoons.

On some waters the angler is very often tormented by insects that bite and unless a precaution has been taken against these winged terrors a fishing holiday can be spoiled. A good dope can be made quite cheaply by mixing the following ingredients, all of which can be obtained at most chemists. Three fluid ounces of pine tar, two fluid ounces of castor oil, one fluid ounce of penny royal and one fluid ounce of citronella oil. Mix all together and allow to simmer over a slow fire for ten minutes then bottle and cork tightly. Not a long job, but it may well save your holiday from being ruined. Smear the dope over face, neck and hands, and it will keep flies away for about three hours when another application should be made. The beauty of this concoction is that it does not irritate tender skins.

When repairing rubber boots, remember to patch them on

the inside instead of the outside. An inside patch will wear longer, be less apt to peel off and looks lots better as well.

Flies that have become bedraggled through constant use can be made to look like new if given a steam bath. The easiest way to do this is to hold the fly with a pair of tweezers in the steam from the spout of a boiling kettle.

If your rubber boots fit too loosely, permitting up and down movement at the heel that usually results in a painful blister, try this idea: soften a cake of paraffin wax by heating it, and coat the inside of the boot heel liberally with it. This eliminates all friction, thus preventing blisters, and makes your socks wear longer.

Metal fly rod rings become worn and serrated after much use and can ruin the finish on a good fly line. To refinish rings so damaged, get some fine emery cloth and tear it into strips about $\frac{1}{8}$ of an inch wide, pass it through the worn rings and draw it back and forth against the worn surface until the ring is smooth. For final polishing use a well-worn strip of emery cloth. Of course, the best way to treat a worn ring is to replace it with a new one.

Pipe-smoking anglers who have lost treasured briars from jacket pockets while fishing needn't suffer such a loss again, Take the clip off an old fountain pen or pencil and slide it on the shank of your pipe; when you put the pipe in your pocket you can clip it there and it will stay put, even when you bend over to net or gaff a fish.

TEN COMMANDMENTS

1. Always carry licence or permit.
2. Be a sportsman at all times.
3. Obey local rules and other regulations as to methods of fishing.
4. Release, carefully, all fish about to spawn and those that have spawned.
5. Be considerate towards other anglers.
6. Kill immediately fish being kept to avoid unnecessary suffering.
7. Report all poachers.
8. Shut all gates on farmland.
9. Check all tackle after a day's fishing.
10. Keep a diary regarding baits used, water and weather conditions and success achieved or otherwise.

INDEX

Names of artificial flies and other artificials, such as nymphs, referred to in the text, are in italics in the Index.

A
alder 35, 83, 84
alevin 15, 16, 87
Alexandra 83, 84, 163, 164
Alexandra and Jungle 168
amadou 44, 45, 58
anti-kink 80, 149
arrowhead 88
artificial baits for salmon 144
artificial nymphs 50 *et seq.*
artificial restocking 19, 85 *et seq.*

B
Baby Doll 99, 100
bailiffs 89
bait fishing for salmon 139 *et seq.*
baits 144
barrel knot 42
beetles 17, 71, 72
Black and Green 163, 164
Black and Peacock Beetle 98, 99, 100
Black Ghost Streamer 148, 149
Black Gnat 83, 84
black nebs 158, 159
Black Palmer 137, 138, 166
Black Spider 35, 36, 83, 84
Black Streamer 98
Black Zulu 164
Blagdon Reservoir 82
blister prevention 185
blood knot 62
bluebottles 71, 72
Blue Charm 129, 137, 138
Blue Dun 34, 35
Blue Dun Nymph 51
Blue Elver 168
Blue Jay 164
Blue Kingfisher 163, 164
Blue and Silver 48, 137, 138, 168
Blue Zulu 84, 163, 164
boiling salmon 154
bones 12
brain size of fish 13
breeding your own worms 64
broiled salmon 155
brown trout 13, 14, 21, 49
Brown Turkey 82
bull trout 113, 114, 115, 178
Butcher 48, 82, 83, 84, 163, 164

C
caddis fly 22, 23, 53
caddis grub 22, 23, 69, 70
Cairns Fancy 82
Canadian pondweed 88
care of rods 91 *et seq.*
care of tackle 91 *et seq.*
casting 55
casting a weighted leader 40
caterpillars 51, 73, 74
celery 89
Chew Reservoir 82
Cinnamon and Gold 82, 83, 163, 164, 166
Cinnamon Sedge 137, 138
Coachman 34, 83, 84
Coch-y-Bondhu 48, 83
Common Shrimp 129, 130, 133
cooking a salmon 154
cooking sea trout 155
Cornwall, flies for, 83
Cranefly 23, 34
creeper 87, 90
creeper fishing 67 *et seq.*
crocodile spinning tackle 180
crowfoot 88, 89
crustaceans 40
Cumbria, flies for, 84
Curry's Shrimp 129, 130, 133

D
daddy longlegs 22, 23
Dam Buster 99, 101
daphnia 16, 87, 89, 90
dapping 72
Dark Olive 83, 84
Dark Olive Nymph 51
Dark Partridge 84
Dark Sedge 83, 84
Deer Hair Streamer 148, 149
demons 48, 51
Derbyshire, flies for, 84
Devil Dodger 82
Devon, flies for, 83
devons 20, 76, 80, 145, 146, 147, 173
dragonfly larvae 16, 17, 87
Durham, flies for, 84
Durham Ranger 103, 128, 129
Dusty Miller 82

E
eel-tail 139, 140, 180
egg 109
estuary fishing for sea trout 171 *et seq.*

F
ferox trout 16
fibreglass rods 92
Fiery Brown 128, 129
fingerlings 85
finnock 158
fish, brain size of, 13
fish foods 86
fish, perception of 11
fishing, night 58, 59, 60
floating lines for salmon 135 *et seq.*
fly fishing for salmon 127
fly fishing for sea trout 163
fiy iines 92
fly maintenance 93
Fly Minnow 51
flies, artificial, history of, 32
flies, number of, 32, 33
fly sizes, salmon 129
foul-hooking 132
Fresh Water Shrimp 51, 90
fresh water shrimp 87
fry 16, 85, 109

G
gaff 125, 134
gammarus pulex 90
gillaroo 18
Ginger Quill 84
Gold-Ribbed Hare's Ear 84
Grannon 84
grasshoppers 71
grayling 12
"greased line" angling 137
Green Corkscrew 139
Greenwell's Fancy 48
Greenwell's Glory 34, 35, 48, 82, 83, 84
Grey Ghost Streamer 148, 149
Grey Turkey 128, 129
grilse 109, 146
grip, rod 57
Grouse and Claret 82, 83, 84, 163, 164
Grouse and Orange 84
Grouse and Yellow 83, 84

H
hackle 36
Hackle Mayfly (Wet) 34
hackles, sparse 37
Hardy's Favourite 84
Hatching Olive Nymph 98, 99
Heather Fly 12, 84
herling 158
herons 31
history of artificial flies 32
holiday fishing 182 *et seq.*
hook shaping 45
hook sharpening 45
hook sizes 11, 12, 23, 33, 48, 72
hooks 43, 45

I
identifying a kelt 116 *et seq.*
identifying a salmon 113 *et seq.*
insect repellants 184
insects, live 71 *et seq.*
Invicta 82
Ireland, flies for, 84
Iron Blue Dun 34, 35, 36, 82, 83, 84
Iron Blue Dun Nymph 51

J
Jeannie 137, 138
Jock Scott 82, 128, 129
Jungle Alexandra 130, 131
Jungle Grub 129, 133
Junglecock and Silver 131, 132

K
kelt 106, 116 *et seq.*
killing a salmon 154
Kingfisher 82, 84
kingfishers 29
knots 62
Knotted Midge 84

L
Lake fishing 46 *et seq.*
Lake Vyrnwy 83
Lancashire, flies for, 84
Large Palmer Fly 57
late spawned trout 18
leader-holder 169
leaders 40, 42, 93
"legs" of fly 36
licences 186
lies 119 *et seq.*, 159, 160
Light Partridge 84
lines 41, 92, 135
live insects 71 *et seq.*
loach 141
loch fishing for salmon 121 *et seq.*
loch fishing for trout 42, 45 *et seq.*
Loch Leven 38, 47, 82, 90
Loch Leven trout 16, 23
Loch Lomond 47, 161
Loch Marie 47
Loch Naver 42
Loch Torridon 111
loch trout 46
"luck" 12

M
maintenance of flies 93
Mallard and Blue 168
Mallard and Claret 48, 84, 163, 164
Mallard and Orange 83, 84

March Brown 33, 35, 36, 48, 82, 83, 84, 164
March Brown Nymph 51
March Brown and Silver 83
March Brown Spider 82
martins 29
maxillary bones 12
mayfly 20, 22, 23, 40, 86
Mayfly (Dry) 34
mayfly hatch 26
Mayfly Nymph 51, 53
"mend" 136
Minnow Fly 51
minnows 16, 17, 40, 72, 85, 90, 163
minnows as salmon bait 141
mollusca 87, 90
molluscs 40
mountain streams 60
multiplying reels 126

N
natural fish foods 86
natural minnow 80
nature, secrets 11
netting 41
night fishing 58, 59, 60
night fishing for sea trout 167 *et seq.*
Northumberland, flies for, 84
number of flies 32, 33
nymphs 29, 35, 40, 50 *et seq.*, 58, 166

O
Olive Dun 83, 84
ova 15
Owl 82
oxygen content of water 20, 25, 48

P
palatal bones 12
Pale Olive 83, 84
parr 109, 110
parr marks 109
Partridge and Orange 83
Partridge and Red 83
Partridge and Yellow 36, 83
Peacock and Silver 168
peal 158
pennell tackle 62, 63
perception of fish 11
Peter Ross 48, 82, 84, 163, 164
Pheasant Tail 83
pipe-loss prevention 185
Plastic and Feather Lure 148
Plastic Flipper Baits 147, 148
Plug Minnow 148
plugs 146, 147
poaching 105, 106, 150 *et seq.*, 186
prawn 139, 140, 143

Q
Quill Minnow 78, 80

R
rainbow trout 13, 14, 23, 24, 95 *et seq.*
Red Palmer 34, 58, 84, 164, 166
Red Spinner 34, 35, 83, 84
Red Spinner Nymph 51
Red Tag 36, 84
reel overhauls 92
reels 42, 56, 92, 126
renovating flies 185
repairing rubber boots 184, 185
restocking, artificial 19, 85 *et seq.*
ribbon weed 89
River Balgy 111, 121
River Chess 38
River Coquet 18, 113, 178, 179, 182
River Derwent 18, 73, 74
River Llugwy 68, 102
River Nith 182
River Tamar 182
River Tavy 58, 160, 182
River Test 101
River Till 18
River Tweed 103, 146, 178, 180, 181
River Urr 18, 56, 151, 152, 172, 182
River Walkham 182
River Ythan 169
rocks, submerged 121
rods 41, 91 *et seq.*, 124
rods, grips 57
Rough Olive 82, 83
rusty hooks 43, 45

S
salmon 102 *et seq.*
salmon fly sizes 129
salmon, identifying 113 *et seq.*
salmon lies 119 *et seq.*
salmon mayonnaise 155
salmon rods 124
salmon steaks 154
Sand-Eel Tail Spinner 140
Scotland, flies for, 84
Scottish loch trout 46
sea trout 114, 115, 149, 157 *et seq.*
sea trout lies 159, 160
Sedge 83, 84
sewin 158
shaping hooks 45
sharpening hooks 45
Silver Doctor 82
Silver March Brown 163, 164
Silver and Red 83
Silver Tip 82, 84
sizes of flies 129
sizes of hooks 11, 12, 23, 33, 48, 72
Sky Pilot 82
smoking salmon 156
smoking trout 95
smolt 109
Snipe and Purple 84
sparse hackles 37

spawn 15, 16, 85, 86
spawning 15, 16, 157, 158
spawning beds 86
Spent Mayfly 34
spinning baits 78 *et seq.*
spinning for salmon 125, 126
spinning for trout 76 *et seq.*
spinning reels 76
Spoons 20, 78, 79, 80, 144, 145
sprat 139, 141
Spring Grub 129, 133
stalking 55
starwort 88, 89
steaming salmon 154
steelhead trout 95
stonefly 22, 23, 53, 86, 90
streamer flies 148, 149
streamers 49, 95
streams 60
"strike" 40, 41, 97
swallow 30
Sweeny Todd 99, 100
"switchover" 136

T
tackle, care of, 91 *et seq.*, 184 *et seq.*
tackle, pennell 62, 63
tarpon 129
Teal 48
Teal and Black 82, 163, 164
Teal and Green 48, 82, 83, 84, 163, 164
Teal and Red 82, 84
Teal and Silver 168
Teal and Yellow 83, 84
terrors 48
Thunder and Lightning 82, 129
toughening worms 64
trolling 47
trout 13, 19, 46, 95, 114, 115
trout feeding area 56
trout smoking 95
trout spawning 15, 16
Tup's Fancy 84

U
upstream worming 61

V
vallisneria 88

W
Waddington Thunder 130, 131
waders 93
wading 59
Wales, flies for, 83, 84
Water Boatman 51
water beetle 17
water crowfoot 88, 89
water-flea 87, 89
water starwort 88, 89
weather 26, 27
weed beds 29
weed, ribbon 89
Welshman's Button 83
wet flies 55
white trout 158
whitling 158
Wickham's Fancy 34, 35, 36, 82, 83, 84
Wilkinson 128, 129
Wilson's Pride 83, 84
winter-kill 16
Woodcock and Hare's Ear 34, 83, 84
Woodcock and Orange 84
Woodcock and Red Hackle 84
Woodcock and Yellow 48, 82, 83
woodlice 72
Woolly Shrimp 129, 130, 133
Worm Fly 51
worms, breeding your own 64
worms for salmon 141, 142, 143
worms, sea trout fishing with, 175 *et seq.*
worms, toughening 64

Y
yearling 16
yellow trout 18
young trout 110

Z
Zulu 48, 84

If you have enjoyed this book, you will also enjoy Bill Davies' six other wonderful paperfront volumes:

FLY DRESSING AND SOME TACKLE MAKING

How to tie your own flies for trout, salmon or sea trout.

BEGIN FISHING WITH UNCLE BILL

A special book for the young fisherman about to take out his rod for the first time.

TECHNIQUE OF FRESHWATER FISHING

The comprehensive manual ideal for every freshwater fisherman.

TECHNIQUE OF SEA FISHING

Boat, rock, beach and pier fishing all fully covered and explained by the maestro from his own experience.

PLACES TO FISH IN BRITAIN AND IRELAND

The wonderful narrative of Bill's thirty years' wandering round the beautiful fishing places of Britain and Ireland.

THE FISH WE CATCH

Based on beautiful drawings from which you can identify your catch, be it freshwater or saltwater fish, or game fish.

All uniform with this book (same price).